What's Happening to Clergy Marriages?

What's Happening to Clergy Marriages?

David & Vera MACE

Abingdon Press
Nashville

What's Happening to Clergy Marriages?

Library of Congress Cataloging in Publication Data

MACE, DAVID ROBERT.
  What's happening to clergy marriages?
  Bibliography: p.
  1. Clergymen's families.   2. Marriage. I. Mace, Vera, joint
author.   II. Title.
BV4396.M32   248.4   80-15814

ISBN 0-687-44867-0

Scripture quotations unless otherwise noted are from the
Revised Standard Version of the Bible, copyrighted 1946,
1952, © 1971, 1973 by the Division of Christian Education of
the National Council of the Churches of Christ in the U.S.A.,
and used by permission.

Scripture quotations noted TEV are from the Bible in
Today's English Version. Copyright © American Bible
Society 1966, 1971, 1976.

MANUFACTURED BY THE PARTHENON PRESS AT
NASHVILLE, TENNESSEE, UNITED STATES OF AMERICA

To Janice and Mahan Siler
Who in their lives and ministry
Model for their friends and colleagues
What a clergy marriage can become

CONTENTS

PREFACE

PART I

Setting the Stage—How This Book
Came to Be Written

PART II

Practical and Situational Aspects—
The View from Outside

PART III

Personal and Interpersonal Aspects—
The View from Inside

60722

PREFACE

This is, to the best of our knowledge, the first book to be written, specifically and exclusively, about clergy marriages. Inquiries we have made have failed to locate another. We hope, however, that it will be followed by many more. The subject is certainly one that needs to be fully ventilated.

Perhaps because this has been something of a pioneer effort, it has been a difficult book to write, and it may be appropriate here to give some of the reasons for this.

First, we encountered difficulty about the term "clergy couple." We discovered that it had been used to describe the marriage in which both the husband and wife are clergy persons—the "two-clergy couple," as we prefer to call it. The term was used in this sense by Richard Hunt in 1976 and again in the report of an Ecumenical Clergy Couple Consultation held in 1978. A thorough exploration of the literature has convinced us, however, that the term "clergy couple" has been used, at least since 1951, to refer to any marriage that includes at least one clergy person. Our decision has been to retain this original meaning of the term.

This issue settled, we then had to look for source material. No comprehensive bibliography on the subject of clergy marriages could be found, so, from all the sources available to us, we compiled our own list of about 120 books, articles, reports, and doctoral dissertations (see Appendix II). We make no claim that this is complete, but it does represent the materials with which we worked in the preparation of our book.

Another difficulty was to decide how far to include historical material. For a large part of Christian history—as long as twelve centuries—clergy marriage was either strongly discouraged or strictly forbidden. We read fairly extensively what literature we could find about the antecedents of today's clergy marriage in the records of the Hebrews, the New Testament, the Early and Medieval Church, and the Protestant Reformation. However, we finally decided that our book should confine itself to contemporary issues, and we therefore reluctantly jettisoned our garnered store of historical material.

The next question was to decide on the level and style of writing. The book is intended primarily for the clergy couples in the United States of America at the present time. But while we realized that many of the persons involved in these marriages would appreciate a book on a scholarly level, we were also well aware that for many others a practical, down-to-earth treatment would be more acceptable. What we have tried to do has been to steer a middle course between these two objectives.

Another issue was that of theological perspective. Married pastors in the United States, as John Scanzoni discovered in his research, exist at both ends of a continuum, but they are also to be found at every intermediate point. In their interpretation of the Bible, their concepts of the authoritarian role of the minister, and their position regarding the hierarchical or companionship concept of Christian marriage, their attitudes exist in what we might call rich variety. Yet surely all are alike in their desire for happy and creative marriages, and our task was, if possible, to meet these needs at this basic level.

With this object in mind we have tried wherever it was appropriate to talk directly, on a couple-to-couple basis, with a representative clergy couple, and in order to be as practical as possible, we have given this couple specific exercises to use for the clarification of their ideas and the improvement of their own relationship. We think the book might be particularly useful to a group of clergy couples meeting regularly for a time to share their ideas and to encourage one another in ongoing relational growth.

We had to set limits to the coverage of the book. We decided therefore not to discuss, except in passing, the quite new situations created by two-clergy marriages and by clergy marriages in which the wife is the minister. We simply lacked sufficient information and experience to be able to arrive at reliable judgments about these new patterns.

We also decided, quite deliberately, not to discuss clergy divorces. We recognize that these confront the churches with difficult and important policy decisions. But our immediate purpose is to do everything possible to prevent clergy marriages from ending in divorce, so we decided to confine ourselves to emphasizing the positive.

Our task in writing this book has been a challenging one. But it has also been rewarding. We have learned a great deal. We have perceived even more clearly than before the importance of this issue for all the churches. Above all, we have been excited at the prospect of ways and means being found to increase the happiness of ministers and their wives across the country, and by so doing to release for them new resources of love and creativity as they pursue their vocations together.

One question to which we naturally sought an answer was, How many clergy couples are there in the U.S.A. at the present time?

We made a rough calculation based on the federal census returns for 1960 and 1970. According to the 1960 figures, about 80 percent of all clergymen were married. We could not make a similar estimate for 1970, because in that year no totals were reported for clergymen, but only for "religious workers." However, the 1970 total for men religious workers was 232,262. If we assume that the great majority of them were clergymen and estimate that 80 percent of them were married, we have a total of about 185,000 clergy couples in 1970. Assuming the same rate of increase in the total number of clergymen between 1970 and 1980 as was recorded for the previous ten years, we come up with a rough estimate of about 220,000 married clergymen in 1980.

We then approached the National Council of Churches of Christ in the U.S.A. and found that their estimate for all clergy serving parishes (there were nearly as many more in other occupations) in 1978 was 271,456. If again we assume 80 percent of them to be married, we have a total of just under 220,000.

These are very rough calculations, based on a number of assumptions that would be very difficult to confirm with any precision. The number would be nearly doubled if we included those clergymen who are not serving parishes, or are retired, who presumably tend not to register as clergymen on the census forms.

Finally, let us express our debt to many people: to the thirty participants in the National Consultation on Clergy Marriage in September 1977; to the many writers and researchers whose materials we have gratefully used; to the clergy couples who have shared their experience of marriage with us; to professional colleagues whose advice and guidance we have sought; to faculty members and library staff at the Southern Theological Seminary in Louisville, Kentucky, where we explored the literature in the field; and to our three typists—Jill Beaver, Shirley Hasty, and Connie Rhoads—who shared the task of producing the final version of the manuscript.

DAVID AND VERA MACE

PART I

Setting the Stage—
How This Book
Came to Be Written

It is striking how seldom books on the Protestant ministry take account of the fact that most ministers are married, with responsibilities as husbands and fathers. The guiding image, after the Protestant Reformation as well as before it, appears to be a celibate priesthood, in which the clergyman gives his undivided loyalty and time to the Church. Few authors meet realistically and constructively the conflicts faced by a minister who seeks to balance the competing demands and responsibilities of his family and his congregation.

William Douglas
in Ministers' Wives, page 260

CHAPTER I

Three Couples in Crisis

The car turned into the driveway and came to a halt at the garage door. Paul Jackson didn't immediately get out. He was aware of a mounting state of anxiety. He had noticed that the downstairs lights of the house were switched off, but the upstairs light was still on. Clearly Sandy had given up waiting for him and had gone to bed. He knew she would be angry and upset. He looked at his watch—it was twenty minutes short of midnight.

Upstairs, Sandy heard the car arrive and braced herself. The simmering resentment within her mounted. She felt her stomach muscles tense up and her fist clench. She remembered her feeling of sick disappointment when Paul had called to say he couldn't get home to dinner. "An emergency situation," he had explained. When she asked what it was, the answer seemed evasive. Something about counseling but, of course, she couldn't ask who, or what, or why? That was forbidden territory to her—the privacy of those counselees must be strictly guarded.

She remembered her blind anger as she laid down the phone. To calm herself, she had gone to her closet for a drink. She had served supper for the children and put them to bed. Then, in the silent, empty house she had waited, hour after hour. Now that Paul had come at last, she didn't know what to do. If she unloaded her anger on him, she knew what would happen. What was the use of trying to explain to him what was going on inside her? He would listen, but he wouldn't hear. Then it would happen all over again—next time.

Paul knew he must go to Sandy and face her wrath, but he felt limp, drained. How tired he was. Yet he had spent himself in a good cause. By staying with them, he had seen a real breakthrough for Alice and Pete. It seemed grimly ironic that he was able to mend the marriages of others while his own went from bad to worse. Somehow he couldn't make Sandy understand that he was a minister of the gospel, and his calling was to meet human need. She was so prejudiced about it.

He had been worried about her lately, though. It was obvious that she was drinking again. He knew he should face her with this, but he also knew how she would react. Her dependency needs were sometimes frightening. How could he meet them when he was constantly in demand? He was worried about the children, too. With Sandy in this bitter, explosive state of mind, he knew they weren't getting the love and care they needed.

Sandy heard the front door open. Paul's footsteps sounded in the hall, then on the stairs. The bedroom door opened, and he stood looking at her. In his eyes she could read perplexity and pain.

Paul and Sandy did not clear up the trouble between them that night. The situation went from bad to worse. Paul would have liked to have sought counseling help, but he couldn't face the cost of acknowledging to others his failure to handle his own life situation.

Sandy's secret drinking became obsessive; it was her only escape from frustration and hopelessness. The crisis came when she took an overdose of sleeping pills and had to be rushed to the hospital. Then the story was out in the open. After her recovery the psychiatrist told Paul very plainly that it might happen again unless he faced up to Sandy's plight. Paul, overwhelmed by a sense of failure and loss of prestige, decided to take drastic action.

He resigned from the ministry, and the family moved out of the community. Paul took a routine job that gave him plenty of time for Sandy and the children. Slowly, over a period of years, they got themselves and the family back on an even keel. Sandy broke her alcoholic habit, and with continued support from Paul she was able to function acceptably as a wife and mother. Paul is still at heart a disappointed man, but he feels he has done his duty and must accept his present situation and make the best of it.

Stan Cooper knew, the moment he saw Kathy, that there was something seriously wrong. She was sprawling over the kitchen table, gazing vacantly into space.

"What in heaven's name is the matter?" he asked.

She was silent for a moment. Then, in a hoarse, frightened voice, she replied, "I've been to the doctor."

"The doctor? What about?"

"For a test. Stan, I'm pregnant."

Stan could feel a welter of emotions rising within him.

"Pregnant? Really, Kathy? Well, why not? That's great news, isn't it?"

"No, Stan, it's bad news. I wish I didn't have to tell you, but—I must have an abortion."

"An abortion? Why, what's the big idea? We want children, don't we?"

Kathy's eyes filled with tears.

"Oh, Stan, I don't know. No, not now. Just as I've gotten started on my career. I can't have a baby—not now, anyway. Maybe never."

"Kathy, what are you saying? You're my wife, aren't you? And this is my child, isn't it? And you talk of killing it—just to keep on with your job? That's awful—just awful! I won't allow you to do such a terrible thing!"

Stan and Kathy were in their middle twenties. He had married her while he was in seminary. It had been a stormy love affair. She had resented his going into the ministry. But Stan had made up his mind to marry her, and he did.

Now in his first church, Stan had hoped that Kathy would find a role for herself as the pastor's wife. She had tried to do so, but she had offended some of the parishioners by her outspoken criticisms of the way they ran the Sunday school. And she had reacted by dropping out. Now she didn't even attend some of the church functions. Stan had put heavy pressure on her to do so, but she had stubbornly refused.

Instead, Kathy had joined a group of artists who were developing a gallery in the community. Stan disliked this, because the people she was associating with were not to his mind appropriate companions for the pastor's wife.

However, Kathy had been an art major, and this was her field, so Stan had let her continue, though he was resentful about it.

Now an opportunity had come for Kathy to take charge of the art gallery and develop the project. She had been excited about this and saw it to be the way to fulfill a cherished dream. Unfortunately, the gallery was to be open on Sundays, which seemed the best day for attracting patrons. This had precipitated a major crisis for the couple. Kathy was not unwilling to have children—but only later, when she had established herself in this new, exciting career.

The conflict grew to major proportions. Stan was strong-willed and assertive. He insisted that Kathy should honor his wishes. At first she appeared to do so. For the sake of peace, she agreed to limit her activities at the gallery, not to go there on Sundays, and have the baby.

But inwardly Kathy couldn't accept Stan's ultimatum. She knew that as the pregnancy developed, an abortion would be more difficult to get.

One day Stan came home to an empty house. A note on the kitchen table informed him that Kathy had had the abortion, was leaving him, and would be living with a young male artist who had befriended her. Stan went berserk, sought out the artist, and a tremendous row followed. In a matter of hours the story was all over town.

In desperation, Stan sought out a senior colleague in the ministry. Every effort was made to patch up the messy situation, but to no avail. Stan couldn't face his congregation again. He left town and later sought a divorce. He is still in the ministry. Intensive counseling has made him aware of some of the mistakes he made. There is a reasonable hope that he will make good in the end.

George Borden picked up the telephone.
"Is that Dr. Borden?"
"Yes, speaking, What can I do for you?"
"You've done more than enough already, and I want an

explanation. This is Arthur Rush—the husband of Nancy Rush."

George felt his throat tighten, and his heart begin to beat wildly. For a moment he was speechlss.

"You have nothing to say, ah? I don't wonder. All right, I have plenty to say. You thought no one would get to know about your affair with my wife, didn't you? Well, you covered it all up pretty cleverly, I'll admit. But what you didn't know was that Nancy talked in her sleep. And when she kept mentioning your name, I got suspicious. So last night I confronted her, and she has confessed everything. A pretty situation for a minister to get into, I must say!"

George sagged limply in his chair. The room seemed to be rotating wildly. He put the phone on the hook and for a moment lost consciousness.

Later that day he had a call from one of his deacons. Arthur Rush had acted as informer, and he must know what Dr. Borden had to say. He expressed the hope that this was just a malicious attack on the part of an unbalanced husband. Quictly, George told the deacon that, unfortunately, the story was true. In a broken voice he said he couldn't understand the way he had acted, but that this looked like being the end of his career as a minister.

Desperately feeling the need to deal with the tumult of his feelings, George got in his car, drove to a nearby town, and booked into a motel. From there he phoned his wife, Cynthia, and told her he had to leave unexpectedly, and he would be back in touch with her soon and explain everything. He tried to phone Nancy at the office where she worked but was told that she was ill and had taken the day off.

The weeks that followed were eventful for George Borden. He met with his deacons and told them the whole story. Nancy Rush had come to him for counseling and unfolded the tale of her miserable marriage to a brutal, tyrannical husband who had beaten her physically. She wanted to leave him but feared for her children. She literally threw herself on George for the sympathy and support she had long needed and the love and under-standing of which she had been starved. The deacons were kind and sympathetic, but they had to point out that what George had done could not easily be overlooked.

One of the deacons, however, took action. He called Arthur Rush and asked him what he planned to do next. When told that, if the whole story came out in the open, his beating of his wife would become public knowledge, he was soon on the defensive. The deacon proposed to make a deal with him. If arrangements were made for Dr. Borden to give up his ministry at the church and quietly leave town, nothing more would be said and the incident would be closed. Arthur Rush agreed to accept this as his revenge.

In a long, anguished session with his wife, Cynthia, George Borden confessed everything with bitter tears and was fully and freely forgiven. There had been some strains in their relationship, and Cynthia saw clearly that she must assume some responsibility for George's vulnerability to the advances of Nancy Rush. Reconciliation between husband and wife was deep and enduring.

As soon as the necessary arrangement could be made, and on the pretext of illness, the Bordens left town. Sometime later, George resumed his ministry by taking a church in another community. We have no information about what happened to Arthur and Nancy Rush.

What went wrong in these three marriages? How did their troubles develop? Should they never have married at all? If the husbands had not been ministers, would the situation have been different? Were the men unsuited to the work of the ministry? Did the women lack what it takes to be clergy wives? Did the congregations place too heavy demands on their pastors or fail to give adequate support to the parsonage families? Could the trouble have been prevented? Could something have been done to avoid final disaster? Are the kinds of situations we see in these particular couples likely or unlikely to arise for ministers generally? What responsibility should ecclesiastical superiors assume when clergy marriages go wrong? Are there measures that could and should be taken to see that unsuitable men (and women) should not be accepted as pastors, or that pastors should not select unsuitable marriage partners?

These and other questions arise whenever a clergy marriage gets into serious trouble, and it seems to be happening more and more often today. Does this mean that the task of the minister is getting tougher? Or is it that troubles of this kind have developed before but were hushed up or otherwise concealed?

Whatever the reason, clergy marriages today seem to be getting into trouble on a scale that demands a full and careful investigation.

CHAPTER II

A Neglected Area of Critical Need

This is a book about Christian ministers and their marriages.

What *is* a minister, and what is he trying to do? The answer is that he is seeking, by every available means, to promote the Christian religion.

What *is* a religion?

It is, above all else, an explanation of the meaning of human life. Either the short span of time we spend on this planet Earth is part of some intelligent design, or it is meaningless, purposeless, futile.

All right, what is the *Christian* explanation of what human life means—its purpose and its goals?

The heart of it is that God, who holds in his hands the power that created us, is wise, good, and loving; that he has a plan that will in the end make all our struggles and sufferings worthwhile; that he has communicated this to us in various ways, but above all in the life and teaching of Jesus of Nazareth; and that through him we have access to resources that can enable us to reflect in our human lives something of the divine love that was revealed in his life, death, and resurrection.

From that point it gets complicated. There are many different interpretations. Yet there is a silken cord that binds all Christians together. In the last resort we would all agree on the two essentials that Jesus summarized in what we call the Great Commandment—that our response to the divine call is to love God, who first loved us, and to love one another because we are all made in his image. Christianity is, above all else, the religion of love.

People who have accepted the Christian message tend to get together in groups; we usually call them congregations. They do this in order to help one another fulfill the Great

Commandment. All congregations together make up the whole body of Christian believers. In the world today there are just about one billion Christians—nearly one-quarter of the human race.

Each small group of Christians tends to appoint a leader, who is set free from other tasks in order to watch over the welfare of the group. The leader's role is described as that of the minister or pastor.

Among the different denominations there has been some disagreement about the qualifications of ministers. Two of these specially concern us here. They are closely related. One was about whether a minister must be of the male sex only. The other was about whether a minister should marry. At different periods of Christian history, there have been different answers to these questions. It is not our task, however, to explore these answers in detail.

This book concerns those branches of the Christian Church that allow ministers to be married and have done so since the Protestant Reformation four hundred and fifty years ago. The Roman Catholic Church has discouraged the marriage of ministers since the third century and strictly forbidden it since the twelfth century. Reasons can obviously be given for this. Being a married minister, and having a family as well as a church to care for, can produce some difficulty.

Marriage is an age-old institution. Christianity has from the beginning seen it as divinely ordained for good and necessary purposes. One of those is to provide a man and woman with an intimately shared life in which they can develop deep love and companionship. In doing this they are coming very close to the essential goal of a Christian life—finding in their love for each other a reflection, and an expression, of God's love for them and their love for God.

A Christian minister's task is to proclaim the message of divine love and to help those who respond to it to grow in love for one another. A married minister can therefore be reasonably expected to provide in his own marriage relationship an image and example of how other people, through their united love for God, can grow in the quality of

23

their love for each other. When a minister's marriage does not demonstrate the warmth and tenderness of human love at its best, an observer could justifiably say, "If his religion doesn't work in this closest of all human relationships, how can we be sure that it is really true?"

That is a searching question—but one that cannot be avoided. Ministers who have poor mariages offer a poor witness to the central message of the gospel.

Wilhelm Pauck in *The Ministry in Historical Perspectives* has expressed this very clearly:

Nothing shaped the social status of the Protestant ministry as decisively as the fact that they were permitted and indeed encouraged to marry . . . . Ministerial households often exemplified the practical application of the Reformers' new understanding of the Christian religion, namely, that the faith in Christ must be practiced in mutual love and service in the natural, social setting of human life and in the ordinary, secular pursuits. Thus the married ministry came to demonstrate that family life together with the manifold social activities it engenders can be a more effective vehicle for religion and the service of God than asceticism, celibacy and other-worldliness. (p. 146)

The married minister with an unhappy marriage is therefore crippled in the performance of his task. He knows that the message he is proclaiming isn't working for him in his own inner personal life. He is not getting, in his home, the healing and support he needs in order to share the burdens of human need and tragedy that are daily brought to him. He suffers from disappointment, guilt, and a sense of failure that leave him inwardly tortured and emotionally drained. His wife also is in trouble. She must either put on an act before the outside world or risk ruining her husband's career by letting the sad truth be known. They both face a grim choice between hypocrisy and public humiliation.

It is terrible and tragic that anything like this should happen to men and women who began with high hopes and noble ideals. It is even more terrible and tragic that the churches they serve should allow these things to happen, averting their eyes until finally, in an increasing number of instances, the tortured clergy couple reach the limits of their endurance and the marriage fails. And then, as the final cynical act, the church stirs and addresses itself to formulating a "policy" to deal with clergy divorces, with little acknowledgment of its lack of concern for the conditions that are causing these divorces.

We are writing this book because we have watched this painful process long enough. We want to reach out, to sound a clarion call, and to offer some workable answers.

We shall have some suggestions to offer to the responsible leaders of the churches. But our real purpose is to talk directly and personally, as a married couple, to clergy couples, to tell them that we have tried to understand their predicament, and above all, to offer them, in clear and specific terms, some answers. As far as possible, we would like to address ourselves directly to clergy couples who are willing to read the book together and to encourage them to put into practice what they see as being relevant to their needs. So we want, right now, to say to them, "As a clergy couple, you deserve a good marriage, and we are going to do everything in our power to make this possible for you."

The World Council of Churches has its headquarters in Geneva, Switzerland. One morning in September 1976, we sat with Leslie Clements in the office of the Department of Family Ministries. We had come to report to him about an inquiry we had been making at his request.

This was familiar ground for us. Back in 1958 we had given a year of service to the International Missionary Council, which was soon afterward united with the World Council of Churches. We had helped to work out a long-term plan for the training of Christian leaders, worldwide, to provide better services to families through the churches. Later we had helped to establish the WCC Department of Family Ministries with Matti Joensuu, a Lutheran pastor from Finland, as its first director—to be followed later by Leslie Clements, a Methodist minister from New Zealand. We, ourselves, continued to serve as consultants in family life to the WCC for about fourteen years.

The inquiry that Les Clements had asked us to carry out had to do with clergy marriages. From several parts of the world the churches were asking for guidance. The first stimulus was usually the shock of seeing ministers and their wives involved in divorce—something that would have been almost unthinkable, and certainly unmentionable, a few years earlier. But it was now impossible any longer to avoid the fact that ministers—only a few as yet, but the number was increasing—were having marital troubles. So Les wrote to us and said, "Would you please investigate this matter for us? What do we really know about clergy marriages? Have there been any studies that could give us information? Have any of the churches developed policies or programs to help clergy couples whose marriages are in trouble?"

As we began to make inquiries, we found that this subject had been given little attention. There were scores of books about the ministry. Seldom, however, did we find anything significant about the minister's marriage. We became accustomed to scanning the chapter headings, then looking up the index under various titles—usually to find nothing at all. When occasionally there *was* a reference, the treatment was usually brief and formal—a few platitudes and nothing more. The idea that a minister's marriage could be in serious trouble, let alone break down, was hardly even hinted at.

There were also some little books written for ministers' wives—one dated as early as 1832. But most of them were full of practical advice on how to meet the expectations of a congregation and made only passing references to the married life of the couple. More helpful were two major studies of clergy wives based on careful research, one by Wallace Denton (1962), the other by William Douglas (1965). Both researches were carried out, however, before the Women's Liberation Movement began to make a major impact on our culture.

In addition, a few good programs have now been developed to provide marriage counseling for clergy couples, and more recently, a few in the new field of marriage enrichment.

Having completed this preliminary survey, our next step became clear. We decided to call a National Consultation on Clergy Marriages.

This took place on September 9-11, 1977, at a retreat center called Wellspring, operated by the Church of the Savior in Washington, D.C. Pastor Don McLanen made all the arrangements, and the National Council of Churches of Christ in the U.S.A. (the Reverend William Sheek) and the Department of Pastoral Care, North Carolina Baptist Hospitals Inc., Winston-Salem, North Carolina (Dr. Mahan Siler) cosponsored the event. We were able to bring together about thirty carefully selected persons, and at last the whole question of the clergy marriage was opened up for investigation. We had no funding, and the report of our deliberations had quite limited circulation. However, a start had been made, and there were encouraging responses from several denominations; although the emphasis for them, all too often, was less upon clergy marriage than upon *clergy divorce*.

It became more and more clear to us that very little is known about the marriages of ministers and their wives. For some years we ourselves deeply engaged in the marriage enrichment movement, have been discovering that many of the clergy couples who came to our weekend retreats had quite superficial relationships. Even those whom we trained for leadership often acknowledged that the greatest benefit of the training experience had been the new growth that got started in their own relationships.

So we came to realize that, behind the front they are compelled to put up for the sake of appearance, many clergy couples have very mediocre relationships. Others live in a state of quiet desperation. They can't disclose their plight to the congregation for fear of being downgraded. They can't go to marriage counselors in their home community because if this became known, it would become an item of local gossip. So they have no alternative but to suffer in silence.

Since we now know the real facts, we are eager to awaken the churches to a realization of what is happening. Our message, however, is much more a positive than a negative one. Many of the couples known to us who were in trouble have now developed happy and creative relationships that are heartwarming to witness. What getting the inside story has done for us, therefore, as this book should make very clear, is to fill us with hope and confidence that, when once we make available to these couples the new insights and resources we now possess for the management of such relationships, the outlook for clergy marriages should undergo spectacular improvement.

That morning in Geneva, in 1976, we tried to sum up our concern about the clergy marriage in a simple, clear statement. Here it is:

If my marriage isn't rich and fulfilling,
   it will be hard for me to be a loving person;
If I don't function as a loving person,
   I cannot be an effective pastor;
If I am not an effective pastor,
   my work will make me increasingly frustrated;
My frustration about my work
   will feed back destructively into my marriage;
This will cause my marriage
   to function less and less effectively;
Therefore, working to achieve a loving and creative
   marriage is a task of major importance for me.

CHAPTER III

What Hundreds of Clergy Couples Told Us

It was October of the year 1962, and the autumn leaves were falling in the mountains of eastern Pennsylvania. When we arrived at Kirkridge, a religious center where we were to spend the weekend with a group of married couples, our condition vacillated between anticipation and apprehension. We had agreed to undertake what was for us an entirely new venture. Although we were at the time the executive directors of the American Association of Marriage Counselors (now the American Association for Marriage and Family Therapy), we had never done anything like this before. Our efforts had hitherto been to deal with marriages that were in trouble; not to help couples with reasonably healthy marriages to keep out of trouble. We had not been able to find any other couple whose experience might have given us some guidance.

However, the weekend went well. And ever since, on an increasing scale, we have been working with couples to help them to improve their relationships. At the same time, we have also been seeking for continuing growth in our own marriage. We have found both tasks to be very rewarding.

While we personally have learned a great deal through seeing the inner workings of hundreds of marriages in this way, we are not free to communicate this knowledge directly, because strict confidentiality is always observed. So we have had to use other means for gathering the information that we now want to share with you. We could do it only through accepted procedures used in research projects.

Beginning in 1976, and having satisfied ourselves that little was known about clergy marriages, we embarked on two new studies of our own. We wanted to know first what the relationships of clergy couples were really like—the inside picture. We also wanted to know how pastors and their wives felt about the clergy marriage as a way of life—its advantages and its disadvantages.

In the rest of this chapter we shall describe, quite briefly, our two studies and what we learned from them. We need to do this because our book is not only a general discussion of clergy marriages. It is also a report on original research of our own, undertaken in order to find answers to our questions. Those of you who want to know about our studies should read on. However, those of you who are interested only in what we found out can omit the next few pages and go straight to chapter 4.

One of the most commonly used research methods is to ask the people you are studying to complete anonymous questionnaires. In our first investigation we did this, but in a special way. There is no need to explain this in great detail, but we do want you to understand the process, so that you can realize what it achieved.

First Study

On five different occasions, covering a period of nearly four years (1976-79), we were invited to lead special conferences for groups of clergy couples. These gatherings lasted from one day and a half to three or four days. Several weeks ahead, we mailed out a package to each of the couples who had registered. It contained two separate forms—a blue one for the husband, a pink one for the wife! On each form the person concerned was asked to check certain items, then put the form in a sealed envelope. They were asked not to collaborate in any way; and the two sealed envelopes were put together in another self-addressed envelope to be returned to us.

What were the questions on the forms? Each had two sections. The pastor's one asked him first to consider a list of areas that had to do with his ministry to families and to check only those areas where he felt he needed further help. Second, he was given another list of seven areas in his own marriage and family and asked to check those in which he felt the need for enrichment. The wife's form also had the same list of seven areas for possible enrichment. The other section on her form listed areas where she might need help in adjusting to her husband's ministry.

It was clear that only areas where help was definitely needed should be checked, but it was also possible to use a double check for an area of special concern.

The five conferences were located in three different states, spanning the eastern half of the U.S.A. The participants represented three Christian denominations—Methodist, Moravian, and Southern Baptist—and served in urban and rural communities in almost equal proportions. Almost all were in the category of "one minister serving one church." The age span was fairly wide, but with an emphasis on the young side. One of the five groups was confined to clergy wives, so there were 113 returns from wives and 87 from husbands—a total of exactly two hundred.

The forms were voluntarily returned—a small number of the conference participants chose not to do so. They were, of course, all anonymously checked, and when we later met with the couples, we had no way of identifying their individual forms. However, the material they gave us was immensely useful in planning the conference programs because we knew exactly what their areas of need were, and we could focus on these. It was also explained to the groups that we would hope to learn from the study what we needed to know about clergy marriages in general.

Remember that these two hundred members of clergy marriages were not a random sample. They had chosen to register for the conferences. This suggests that they were, on the whole, couples who were sufficiently interested to participate in programs dealing with marriage and family issues. We are not sure how other couples who chose not to come would differ from these.

We are, however, somewhat skeptical about so-called "random" samples. It is rare indeed, when questionnaires are mailed out, for more than a proportion of them to be returned. And when invitations to be interviewed are issued, it is also highly probable that some will decline,

31

unless pressure is used to get them to come, in which case their sincerity is in question.

Anyway, enough of explanations. You are eager to hear what we learned about these clergy marriages.

The best way in which we can report what these two hundred people told us is by listing the items in terms of the frequency with which they were checked.

We will omit the areas in which the pastors needed help in their ministry to other families, because, although this is interesting, it is not of primary concern to us in this book. So first, we will give you the areas in which these clergy husbands and wives were in need of personal help in their marriage relationships. You will find these in Table I.

TABLE I
AREAS OF NEED FOR FAMILY ENRICHMENT

Items Anonymously Checked by Four Different Groups of Pastors and Wives, and One Group of Wives Only. Overall Percentages.

Item	Pastors	Wives
1. Handling Negative Emotions (Anger, etc.)	50%	69%
2. Couple Communication	50%	62%
3. Family Devotions	40%	55%
4. Resolving Conflict	42%	46%
5. Separateness and Togetherness	35%	41%
6. Social Life and Recreation	24%	43%
7. Expression of Affection	37%	32%
8. Discipline of Children	24%	27%
9. Sex Relations in Marriage	21%	23%
10. Husband-Wife Roles and Status	19%	24%
11. Money Management	13%	27%
12. Decision Making	16%	20%
13. Aged Parents	13%	19%
14. In-Laws and Relatives	5%	14%

Second, you will find the areas in which the clergy wives needed help in adjusting to the circumstances of their husbands' ministry. These are given in Table II.

TABLE II
CLERGY WIVES—HELP NEEDED IN THEIR ADJUSTMENT TO THEIR HUSBANDS' MINISTRY

Items Anonymously Checked by Five Different Groups of Clergy Wives. Overall Percentages.

1. Need for Time Alone Together	68%
2. Understanding Role of Pastor's Wife	48%
3. Wife's Role in Husband's Counseling	44%
4. Friends Outside the Church	40%
5. Wife's Status in the Church	39%
6. Privacy in Family Life	32%
7. Wife Taking an Outside Job	31%
8. Cooperation in Household Chores	30%
9. Cooperation in Raising Children	28%
10. Attitudes to Women's Liberation	20%

What we would ask you to do at this point is simply to look at all these responses in a general way. But if as a couple you really want to get into the act yourselves, it might be worthwhile for you to copy out the list in Table I, and then separately, without collaboration, check the items in the order in which they represent your personal needs. Try not to be influenced by the order in which the other couples listed them.

Then, when you have made your personal lists, share them with each other, noticing any important differences between you. You might then want to compare your needs with those of the clergy couples who participated in our investigation. This experience will help you to start looking at your own clergy marriage, and you may gain some new insights from doing so.

We shall, of course, be discussing these areas of need in detail throughout the book. But next we have another study, of a somewhat different kind, to report to you.

Second Study

In addition to identifying the special needs of clergy couples in their adjustments to each other, we wanted to find out how they felt about clergy marriage as a special and unique kind of relationship. So we carried out another study to get this information.

This time we did not send out questionnaires, although again we used groups of couples who attended retreats and conferences, which we led. Our procedure this time was to ask them, without previous warning, to take about fifteen minutes to write down spontaneously, and without any collaboration, a list of the advantages, and then of the disadvantages, of the clergy marriage. We gave them no lists to work on, but asked them to select items from their own personal experience and observation, and to write down separately all the positive, and then all the negative, items that came into their heads. The lists were of course anonymous, and we collected them up when they were completed. After the written lists had been turned in, we provided some opportunity for discussion, either all together, or in small groups, or both. We put up the results of their corporate thinking on the chalkboard in a call-in session and kept these for the record.

This second investigation was carried out in three different conferences. One of them overlapped with a group where the earlier questionnaire study was used, and this helped to provide some basis of comparison. The other two conferences were entirely separate and held in different geographical areas—one in the Eastern United States and one in the West. This part of our investigation added another 79 pastors and 42 wives to the number of participants, making a total for both studies of 166 husbands and 155 wives, a grand total of 321 persons. We also picked up ten responses from laypersons who were participating in one of the conferences. These were interesting, but, of course, too small and select a group to warrant inclusion in the study.

This way of getting information was experimental. We had never heard of such a method being used before. The items that had been written down were entirely the personal and original ideas of those concerned. There had been no time for them to prepare, and there was no opportunity to consult with anyone else, or to make changes after learning what others thought. This seemed, for our purpose, much better than questionnaires, which would have imposed our own ideas on the group and left them no opportunity to include items of their own except on an add-on basis. By combining the three separate lists, we felt we gained a fairly representative picture of how pastors and their wives view the advantages and the disavantages of the clergy marriage.

Of course, it took a lot of work to go through a total of two lists each from 168 persons (husbands and wives who took part in this second study), decide from their own language what they were trying to say, identify items that kept recurring, and then find the totals for each item. Actually it didn't prove to be as difficult as it sounds; it was soon clear that many of the participants were saying substantially the same things in different words. Of course, there is a small margin of error, but we are entirely satisfied that we were able to find out what the big issues are, which was what we had hoped for.

The lists of advantages and disadvantages that were most frequently mentioned by the three groups combined appear on the following pages, 36 and 37. The list of advantages is in Table III and the disadvantages in Table IV.

You might like as a couple to sit down separately for fifteen minutes and make your personal lists of the advantages and disadvantages of the clergy marriage as you have experienced and observed them. Then compare your lists with each other and with the lists put together by the couples in our groups.

What we are going to do, in most of the rest of this book, is to try to understand what these hundreds of clergy couples were trying to tell us about themselves. And, of course, we shall feel free also to draw on our years of working with yet more hundreds of clergy couples with whom we have shared in marriage enrichment experiences, though we cannot report directly anything they have told us.

TABLE III
ADVANTAGES OF CLERGY MARRIAGE

Items Anonymously Listed by Three Groups of Pastors and Wives. Overall Percentages.

Item	Pastors	Wives
1. Shared Christian Commitment and Spiritual Resources	63%	56%
2. Unity of Purpose in Ministering to Others	44%	66%
3. Nurturing Support of Congregation	47%	50%
4. High Status, Respect in Community	40%	40%
5. Wife's Close Identification with Husband's Work	30%	50%
6. Meet Interesting People, Travel, Conferences	23%	38%
7. Opportunities for Study, Training, Growth	28%	30%
8. Challenge to Model Christian Family	29%	27%
9. Ready-made Community of Friends	24%	31%
10. Counseling Role Satisfies, Gives Insight	34%	14%
11. Flexible Schedule Aids Family Plans	22%	20%
12. Gifts and Services from Congregation	14%	23%
13. Creative Work, Job Security	19%	13%
14. Support from Colleagues, Denomination	12%	20%
15. Being "Change Agents" in Church and Society	6%	9%
16. Clergy Husbands Are Specially Helpful	0%	13%
17. Living Standards Acceptable	6%	6%
18. Receive Strokes for Good Work Done	9%	2%
19. Housing Is Provided with Job	3%	5%

In our preparation for writing this book, we have also drawn on a number of related studies—in particular those of Denton, Douglas, Fairchild and Wynn, Mattis, Presnell, Scanzoni, Troutner, and van Arnold. These can be identified from the List of Sources at the end of the book. We also located several small questionnaire studies—for example, those of Hayes, and one carried out by the Academy of Parish Clergy. We were gratified to discover that the findings from these other investigations agreed very closely with our own, and we would therefore venture to claim that this book is based on the most accurate information available about clergy marriages at the present time.

We would, however, express the hope that a much more extensive study of clergy marriages can soon be carried

TABLE IV
DISADVANTAGES OF CLERGY MARRIAGE

Items Anonymously Listed by Three Groups of Pastors and Wives. Overall Percentages.

Item	Pastors	Wives
1. Marriage Expected to Be Model of Perfection	85%	59%
2. Time Pressures Due to Husband's Heavy Schedule	52%	55%
3. Lack of Family Privacy—"Goldfish Bowl"	52%	38%
4. Financial Stress—Wife Must Seek Job	34%	36%
5. No In-Depth Sharing with Other Church Couples	22%	48%
6. Children Expected to Model Church's Expectations	25%	39%
7. Husband, Serving Others, Neglects Own Family	27%	25%
8. Role Expectations Suppress "Humanness" of Pastor and Wife	21%	25%
9. Wife's Duties Assigned by Church: She Feels Exploited	20%	21%
10. Emotional Stress Caused by Crisis Situations	17%	21%
11. Unfair Criticism from Church Members	13%	19%
12. Confusion About Wife's Identity and Roles	9%	19%
13. Dissatisfaction with Housing Arrangements	11%	16%
14. Frequent Moves: No Permanent Roots	14%	13%
15. Husband "On Call" Throughout 24 Hours	9%	17%
16. Family "Belongs" to Congregation	9%	11%
17. Husband Must Work When Others Are Free	11%	8%
18. Peer Pressure to Conform and Compete	12%	3%
19. No One "Ministers" to Clergy Family	9%	5%

out. A reseach project of the dimensions of the Douglas study, which covered three years and was generously funded, would provide us all with vitally important information.

It is also our hope that by sharing all this material with you and asking you as a couple to share it with each other, we shall begin to find some answers that may be helpful to you personally. And we will try to persuade the churches generally to develop new policies and programs that will enable the clergy not only to be happier in their marriages, but also to be able to fulfill more harmoniously their dual obligations to their churches and to their families.

CHAPTER IV

What Are the Real Issues?

What we are now going to do is to look back over the mass of material we reported on in the last chapter and to pick out of it the concerns that keep being expressed. You may have your own ideas about what's happening in clergy marriages, and we certainly have ours. But at this point we are going to listen carefully to the hundreds of people who have contributed to all of the studies we have reported, and see what they are trying to tell us.

You will not have to keep checking back to the tables—we'll do that for you. It will be best to follow the same order as we used in the last chapter, beginning with the items checked by husbands and wives, which expressed their needs for enriching their own marriages and their family life.

Notice first that all except one of the items were checked more often by women than by men; suggesting that clergy wives are having more trouble, generally, than their husbands are. The sole area in which the husbands are in greater difficulty is in the expression of affection.This is not confined to clergymen. It is equally true of husbands generally in our culture, and it reflects what has been described by a British psychiatrist, Ian Suttie, as the "taboo on tenderness." It seems to affect particularly the males of the species! This was certainly true in our marriage though we have now gone a long way toward overcoming it.

Notice also that while about one-third of all husbands and wives are having difficulty in expressing their positive feelings toward each other, they are having even more trouble with their negative feelings. Half of the husbands, but two-thirds of the wives acknowledge such difficulty. This is entirely in keeping with our personal observation—struggling with anger is a frequently occurring experience among the clergy couples we have worked with. Of course, pastors and their wives would feel that it was imperative to suppress their anger except in complete privacy. So nothing would show on the surface. But the emotional and spiritual damage that results from all this bottled-up anger and frustration can be devastating.

These couples are not much better off in the area of *communication*. Half of the husbands, and nearly two-thirds of the wives, are having trouble here. Nearly half of both, also, are *unable to resolve conflict* in an acceptable manner.

These are vital areas for a truly happy and successful marriage. Of course all these deficiencies are carefully concealed by the couples concerned. If the couples in our study are representative, however, this means that half of all ministers and their wives are dissatisfied with their attempts to communicate effectively, to manage their negative feelings, and to resolve their conflicts successfully.

Another item high on the list is *family devotions*. We would have to concur that many clergy couples are baffled and perplexed about how to worship together in the home. The wives, consistently, seem more troubled about this than the husbands, perhaps because it falls mainly to their lot to get the children to cooperate.

More than a third of the couples are having difficulty with *"separateness and togetherness"*—the task of balancing individual freedom with the needs and obligations of the shared life. This issue has grown in significance in recent years with the joint impact of the "do your own thing" movement and of Women's Liberation. It is linked somewhat with the issue of husband-wife roles and status, which occurs a little further down the list.

Concern about *social life and recreation* is a good deal stronger with wives than with husbands, though it is an issue for both.

About a quarter of the couples are dissatisfied with their handling of *child discipline*. Incidentally, we found this to be a bigger issue for clergy couples living in urban communities than for their rural colleagues.

The checking of *sex relations* is a very consistent item. There was very little variation from group to group, or between husbands and wives. As far as they are able to admit it, one in five seems to need help in this area. Notice, however, that *sex is a relatively minor item compared with anger!* Who would have expected this in clergy couples?

Money management comes fairly low on the list, though it is causing the wives twice as much concern as the husbands. It must be remembered, however, that these studies were mostly made before raging inflation overtook us. We shall see later that the need of many couples is for more money to manage!

Finally, notice that *in-law troubles are far down on the list.* Time was when in-laws were considered a major cause of marital trouble. No longer. But notice that the wives are three times as much concerned about it as the husbands.

We may turn now to the difficulties listed by the wives as they try to adjust to the special conditions of being married to ministers.

Prominently at the top of the list is the need for "time alone together." Two-thirds of all the wives have checked this, and we shall find it recurring again and again.

Half of the wives are confused about just what they are expected to do. We are all aware today that the roles of wives in general are rapidly changing, and evidently there is additional confusion about the roles of the wives of ministers. The item about the wife's status in the church is closely related to this.

It may seem surprising that the wife's relationship to the pastor's counseling role is so high on the list. However, we know that the involvement of ministers in counseling is rapidly increasing today, and wives obviously have some concern about this.

Friendships outside the church have also been a perplexing matter for clergy wives, and inevitably this is linked with the question of taking an outside job. For those who do so (about half of them now, it is reported), cooperation from the husband, in household chores and child raising, obviously becomes an important question.

The issue of privacy, or the lack of it, in the pastor's family life can be counted on to come up again and again. It is linked mainly with the parsonage system. We shall see later that many husbands, as well as wives, are upset about this.

Taking these responses as a whole, we get a rather disturbing picture of the clergy wife carrying a heavy load. Denied adequate time for maintaining the intimate relationship with her husband, she often feels lonely and frustrated. Add to this a great deal of confusion about what exactly the congregation expects of her. Then there is the feeling of uncertainty about developing friendships outside the church; and, if she feels she ought to take an outside job or wants to do so, she must consider how far her husband can be counted on to share the homemaking duties. Add all this together, and we begin to understand why she has so much difficulty handling her negative emotions.

We must now consider the findings of the second study. Since our attention has been focused on the areas of difficulty and need, it would probably be best to look first at *disavantages* of the clergy marriage (Table IV) and leave the more positive side till later in the chapter.

Our couples have given us a long list of negative items—nineteen in all. Of course there were many others, mentioned only a few times, but these we are not attempting to deal with.

A careful analysis of this material, and comparison with other studies, show that the complaints fall into three major areas.

First, clergy couples are almost obsessed with *the feeling that they are expected to be superhuman and to provide models for the congregation and the community.* For both husband and wife this is the top item; in the husband's case, it is no less than 23 percentage points *above any other.* Clergy couples find that those idealistic expectations generate in them feelings of guilt and rebellion, which are depressing and at times paralyzing. This is without question a major issue, and we shall have to look at it very thoroughly. Here it is related particularly to expectations for the clergy marriage as such. But the burden is increased by other and wider aspects that appear on the list. Item 6 refers to expectations of how the children ought to behave; Item 8 to the role expectations that both husband and wife feel are imposed upon them individually; Item 9 to the feeling of the wife that her duties in the church are subtly imposed, denying her freedom of choice; Item 11 to the pain and injustice of criticisms from church members whose expectations are not met; Item 16 to the feeling that the family "belongs" to the congregation, and must fulfill its requirements; Item 18 to the husband's sense of pressure to meet the standards demanded for "success" in the ministry. Of course, all vocations demand the meeting of stated requirements; but for the ministry, as it is at present constituted, this seems to be particularly so.

Closely allied to this is the second major item *concern about lack of privacy.* Clearly they are interrelated. The need for privacy is the desire not to be observed by eyes believed to be critical and probing for faults. This concern finds expression in a chorus of complaints about the parsonage system.

The third major area is one of great concern. It includes *the heavy work schedule that the pastor has to confront and the time pressure that constantly assails him.* We have already seen that the clergy wife's greatest need is for time alone together, and we find this repeated in item 7 in her complaint, shared fully by her husband, that while serving others he is placed in the position of neglecting his own family. Not only is his time consumed by his work, but Item 10 reminds us that he must deal with poignant human situations involving tragedy and grief, and that doing so is, and must be, emotionally exhausting. There is also the factor listed in Item 15, that he is hardly ever able to relax totally, because his availability to deal with human need covers the entire twenty-four hours of the day. The time frame is further referred to in Item 17, where we are reminded that the period when the minister is most busily engaged—weekends and evenings—covers the very hours when most other workers, with their families, are free to rest and relax.

Further, Item 4 draws attention to the fact that the pastor, his time consumed by prodigious labors, is not in general paid for his work on a scale commensurate with people in other vocations who put in less time and are no better qualified.

Several of the items are of particular concern to the clergy wife. The inability to develop close relationships with other couples in the church, lest this should be interpreted as discrimination and favoritism, troubles half of the wives but only one in five of the husbands. Wives are naturally specially concerned about what the unreasonable expectations of the congregation and community do to the children. The wife is also twice as disturbed as her husband by the confusion about her identity and roles.

Taken by itself, this could be seen as a grim picture. It certainly raises some serious questions and helps to explain why clergy couples have to struggle with a lot of anger and other negative feelings. However, this is of course, by design, only one side of the coin. There are compensations, and they are substantial. So we had better now look at them. They are listed in Table III.

It is interesting that the nineteen disavantages, referred to often enough to be listed, happen to be balanced by nineteen *advantages*. If the task of the ministry is demanding, the rewards are also considerable; and potentially at least, this is specially true for the married minister.

Topping the list are two items that are closely related. The first is *the sense of shared commitment* to the pastoral vocation and the *spiritual resources on which the couple can draw* as they face this heavy task. Second is the *strong sense of unity* that comes from a side-by-side and hand-in-hand dedication together to *a life of service to others*. There is plenty of evidence, in all walks of life, that the service-oriented philosophy is the most fulfilling one and that often what most effectively unites husband and wife is to be engaged in jointly ministering to human need. This is reflected again in Item 5, the wife's close identification with her husband's work; in Item 13, the relatively creative and secure nature of the job; in Item 15, the satisfaction of being "change agents"; and in Item 18, the "strokes" from others that result.

Next in order comes the *nurturing support of the congregation.* This stands in sharp contrast to the unreasonable expectations and demands listed under "disavantages." It is reinforced in Item 9—the fact that a ready-made community of friends is provided, which is specially welcome as the couple move into a new parish. Item 12 gratefully acknowledges also the gifts and services that come from the congregation and community. There is even a small word of appreciation in Item 19 for the parsonage, and a handful of couples even regard the living standard as acceptable!

Other benefits come more indirectly. Item 4 refers to the high status of the clergy in the community; Item 6 to the chances to travel, attend conferences, and meet interesting people; Item 7 to opportunities to learn and study and to be involved in group experiences; Item 14 to support from other clergy couples and from denominational resources.

Some on-the-job benefits are also gratefully recognized. The pastors generally find their counseling role satisfying; though we have noted that the disparity in the responses of the wives suggests a decided difference of opinion here! There is also some acknowledgment that though the job is tough, the flexible schedule gives the pastor special freedom to meet family needs.

It is particularly interesting that Item 8 presents a positive aspect of the major complaint listed among the disadvantages—seeing the high expectations of the congregation as a challenge to live up to the standards expected of a Christian family; and it is worthy of note that more than one-quarter of both husbands and wives view it in this perspective.

Indeed, perhaps the most interesting fact about most of the evaluations is the way in which item after item has both a negative and a positive aspect; and it seems to be the perspective in which each issue is seen that makes the difference. The high expectation of the congregation can be viewed as either judgment or challenge. The burdens of the work are compensated for by the fruits that it may yield. The joy of caring for people in distress leads unavoidably to emotional exhaustion. The pressures applied by congregational demands are at least partially mitigated by nurturing support and individual deeds of kindness.

It could be commented that this is simply what life is all about. You have to take the rough with the smooth, the highs with the lows, the cons with the pros. But that could be oversimplification and evasion. There are seemingly real injustices here, even if they are less real than imagined. There are situations that, with a little sensitivity and imagination, could be changed for the better. It is necessary to find ways to make the advantages seem more real and the disadvantages less odious. As a familiar prayer expresses it—to change what can be changed, to accept what can't, and to be wise enough to know the difference.

In the rest of the book we shall explore in detail the issues we have identified in this chapter. In Part II the focus will be on difficulties that pastors and their wives meet in coping with the demands and pressures of the environment in which they have to live and of the tasks they have to perform. These are the difficulties that seem to arise from *outside themselves*. Then, in Part III, we shall focus our attention on the adjustments that become necessary in their struggle to achieve their own personal and interpersonal goals. These are the difficulties that arise from *inside themselves*. This happens not to be the order in which we collected our material, as described in chapter 3. But it seems to us to be the logical way of dealing with the issues as we now proceed.

PART II

Practical and
Situational Aspects—
The View from Outside

CHAPTER V

The Congregation Expects . . .

To: The Reverend Joseph Andrews
From: Bethany Church, Sometown, U.S.A.

On behalf of the officers and congregation, we welcome you and Mrs. Andrews to our church and look forward to a time of great blessing under your ministry. We take this opportunity of presenting to you this Declaration of Expectations, which has been unanimously accepted by all the officers and approved at a congregational meeting.

Here are our expectations:
You will, as our pastor, set us all an example of Christian living. You will be a model to us of Christ-like behavior in everything you say and do.

You will in your preaching faithfully declare the gospel message in full and strict accord with the teaching of the Bible.

You will perform faithfully all the duties of the pastoral office—calling on sinners to repent, visiting the sick, comforting the afflicted, and building up the congregation in faithful adherence to the principles of Christian living.

In your life in our community, you and your family will have no associations with men and women of evil character, take no part in ungodly activities, frequent no places of worldly pleasure or entertainment.

Your homelife will provide us all with a model of a truly Christian family. No harsh words or unloving acts will take place between you, your wife, or your children.

Mrs. Andrews will be regular in attendance at all worship services and congregational functions. She will provide

leadership for our women's organizations and set an
example as wife and mother for all the ladies of the church.
She will be a gracious hostess on all occasions when
entertainment is provided for members of the congregation
in the church or in the parsonage.

As parents, you will demonstrate to us all how children
should be brought up in the nurture and admonition of the
Lord, and your children will serve as models of good
behavior in the church and in the community.

If you and your family faithfully fulfill these expectations,
you may be assured of our full and loyal support so long as
you continue to be our pastor.

Did you ever hear of a document like this being
presented to any minister as he became the pastor of any
church? Neither did we!

Yet many clergy couples have shared with us feelings,
ranging from apprehension to anger, which suggest that
this might well have happened to them. Here are some
examples, taken from our inquiry into the disadvantages of
clergy marriage:

"Pressure to live up to the image other people have of the
pastor and his family."
"The awareness that all you do is being observed for
good or bad."
"Feeling that it is a sin to make a mistake."
"Always being expected to be a model couple."
"Congregation has expectations about our behavior."
"Too much expected of us by congregation and
community."
"Unreal expectations from the laity."
"We are put on a pedestal and expected to be almost
perfect."
"We are expected to be picture perfect."
"The sense of being watched makes you feel inhibited."

These are just a few picked at random. Remember that 85
percent of all the husbands and 59 percent of all the wives
listed this item.

Remember, too, that 52 percent of husbands and 38 percent of wives listed a lack of privacy. People can have many reasons for wanting privacy. One of them surely is that they don't want their behavior to be observed, because they fear that what they do will be disapproved of. Many of our respondents said they wanted to be "free to be human." One pastor said, "I want to be able to blow my top once in a while." A wife said she couldn't be on her best behavior all the time; another wife—"When I yell at the children, I'm afraid someone may hear me."

What is going on here? Are congregations really putting this kind of pressure on pastors and their families? We greatly doubt it.

Yet the pressure is there all right. Who is misunderstanding what? Who is confusing or deceiving whom?

Let us consider some of the sources from which these supposed expectations could be coming. We see them as falling into five interconnected categories.

1. Traditional Attitudes to the Pastor as Head of a Family.

We need to remember that, until very recent times, the father was an authoritarian figure who made all major decisions for his family and who could therefore be held directly responsible for the way in which the family members behaved.

When Joshua declared to the assembled leaders of Israel, "As for me and my house, we will serve the Lord" (Joshua 24:15b), he did not mean he had discussed the matter with his wife and children, and they had come to a joint decision. He had simply *decided for them.* That was his duty and his right.

This traditional attitude still dominated the churches in 1829, when Charles Bridges wrote these words: "A family is a small diocese, in which the first essays are made of the Episcopal and Ecclesiastical zeal, piety, and prudence. If therefore 'a man know not how to rule his own house, how shall he take care of the Church of God?' (I Tim. 3:12). For he cannot reasonably expect to perform in his parish the work, which he has not cared to acomplish at home" (p. 154).

Hartzell Spence, in his book *One Foot in Heaven*, tells the story of his father's ministry in Iowa in the early days of the present century (about one hundred years after Bridges wrote). He describes how the life-style of the preacher's family was expected to be modeled on the Methodist *Discipline*. There was to be no work done on Sunday, no intoxicating liquor, no motion pictures, theater, or professional entertainment, no dancing or tobacco, no card games, no singing of "secular" songs or reading of "secular" books. Looking back in 1940 he wrote:

> If these stringent church rules were rigidly enforced, the Methodists would indeed be a small society. However, only the preachers and their families are expected to abide by them. My sister and I . . . found it hard to understand why we could not play the games that the Sunday-school superintendent's children enjoyed. When we bought our first phonograph we saw no sin in a charming record called "Toddling," but father smashed it over his knee. Very often, when we children went out of bounds and violated precepts, mother glossed over our crimes. (p.37)

Although most of these very strict rules seem today to be no longer insisted upon by The United Methodist Church, or by most other denominations, it seems that the same basic concept—that there is one standard for the minister's family and another for the laity—still survives.

2. Traditional Attitudes to the Pastor's Wife.

There are two aspects of this, related, but worthy of separate consideration.

First is the wife's social bahavior. Again, Bridges gives us the picture as it was in 1829. The pastor's wife is expected to exhibit

> gravity, self-control, sobriety of deportment, and faithful exhibition of relative and public duties. . . . The woman, having promised obedience to her husband, can do nothing but what he

either directs or approves. . . . The wife of a Minister, if she is inclined to the world, will preach worldly compliance with more success by her conduct, than her husband can preach the renunciation of the world by the most solemn discourses. (pp. 156-57)

Many of the early books written for clergy wives during this century provide precise information on how to dress, what to say and what not to say, how to behave toward this or that person; in fact, some books have whole chapters on etiquette for the pastor's wife.

Here, for example, is a quote from Lucille Lavender's book *They Cry, Too! What You Always Wanted to Know About Your Minister But Didn't Know Whom to Ask.*

A minister's wife should be attractive, but not too attractive; have nice clothes, but not too nice; have a nice basic hair-do, but not too nice; be friendly, but not too friendly; be aggressive and greet everyone, especially visitors, but not too aggressive; intelligent, but not too intelligent; educated, but not too educated; down-to-earth, but not too much so; capable, but not too capable; charming, but not too charming. (p. 89)

Of course, this was written in 1976, and is clearly a tongue-in-cheek statement. But it is not far removed from other advices offered to the pastor's wife in dead earnest.

The second aspect of the traditional attitude to the pastor's wife is the expectation that she will automatically assume the assistant-pastor role.

There can be no doubt that, in the past, the minister's wife was generally expected to take on certain duties. These were not specifically defined, and varied to some extent from congregation to congregation. Again Hartzell Spence describes for us how it was in Methodist churches in Iowa in the early years of this century.

Mother worked in the parish and taught Sunday-school class. She led the devotions before the missionary societies. She played hostess to the Ladies' Aid, the Sew and So Club, and the Committee for the Alleviation of the Plight of the Poor. Feminine complaints too delicate for the pastor's ear came to her, and she bolstered the sisters in all their hours of trial. She sat by sickbeds, comforted widows, consoled jilted and betrayed maidens, heard an unending stream of petty personal complaints. She was a psychiatrist before the days of psychiatry. . . .

How she did it is a mystery that no one but another minister's wife can ever understand. (p. 35)

Historically, the assistant pastor role gradually emerged as ministers began to marry educated and talented women. Many pastors' wives really enjoyed the involvement in their husbands' work that became possible for them and found it fulfilling and rewarding. Others, however, felt it to be a heavy burden and imposed upon them.

Now, this role is gradually being phased out, as more and more pastors' wives find it necessary to take outside jobs or choose to follow independent careers. But in many churches the traditional expectations still linger.

Two things seem to be quite clear. First, any woman who marries a minister with no real sense of sharing in his vocation is going to create a difficult situation for both of them. Second, the minister's wife should be under no compulsion to meet congregational expectations that are unwelcome and uncongenial to her, and her husband should firmly support her in confining herself to whatever roles in the church she can comfortably and happily accept.

Since our concepts of the role expectations of the pastor's wife are changing today and since this can lead to misunderstanding and confusion, we would strongly recommend that, when a pastor receives a call to a new church, an agreement concerning duties and expectations (very different, needless to say, from the one with which this chapter began!) should be drawn up before the call is finally confirmed, and this agreement should include a statement about the expected role of the pastor's wife, as defined and accepted in a conference in which she herself has taken part.

3. Zealots and Malcontents in the Congregation.

Our investigations, though not very thorough, have consistently given us the impression that lay members of congregations are generally charitable and well disposed toward the minister and his family. In many churches, however, there exist certain members who, by their fault finding and belligerence, communicate to the pastor, and particularly to his wife, an impression about the views and attitudes of the congregation that is largely or entirely inaccurate.

Kathleen Nyberg in *The Care and Feeding of Ministers* has described these troublesome church members. "The church is the one place where all are welcome. . . . [It] will always be a mixture of the difficult and the dear. . . . The church is the one public place in the world where one can vent one's gall, relieve one's frustrations, reveal one's distortions, and still expect to be heard." And in *I Married a Minister*, edited by Golda ElamBader, Ruth Levi, a rabbi's wife, vividly illustrates the way in which carping criticism can be directed against the minister's wife.

If she is brilliant or militant or persuaded of her ability to be a leader, she is likely to be considered forward, aggressive; if she is timid, hesitant, or just convinced that it is wiser that only her husband's voice should be raised in the market place, she will be called stupid or lacking in initiative. If she . . . [is] lovely to look upon—she will be said to be vain and frivolous; if she considers extreme stylishness trivial and unworthy the time it requires, her critics will pronounce her dowdy, "old-timey," obsolete. (p. 171)

It is, therefore, a wise plan for the pastor and his wife to make sure that they know where the expectations and the criticisms are really coming from.

4. Pressures from Ecclesiastical Colleagues and Superiors.

The evidence we have found has convinced us that the ministry in the U.S.A. is a highly competitive system, squarely based on the American success syndrome. From the moment he places his foot on the lowest rung of the ladder, the young pastor is constantly encouraged to climb upward to higher and higher levels of the hierarchy. The rewards come in terms of recognition, status, and salary. The credits are awarded for skill, popularity, and hard work. The evidences of worth consist mainly in increasing congregational membership, raising money, putting up buildings, and achieving favorable publicity by whatever means.

A dedicated minister can ignore the system, and success may come to him unbidden. Here and there competitive aspects of the system have been eliminated, as in the Adventist principle of paying all the pastors equal salaries. Bu we suspect it may be very hard not to get involved in the system, because it operates with great subtlety.

The question that concerns us, however, is whether these pressures apply significantly to a pastor's family situation. Our opinion is that they do, but that their operation is negative rather than positive.

As long as a pastor projects the appearance of being a reasonably normal husband and father, all is well. Having a talented or beautiful wife, or highly successful children, will gain him some extra credit. But the crunch comes on the deficit side. A pastor who develops problems in his family life is significantly downgraded. A pastor involved in separation or divorce, apart from a few very atypical exceptions, plummets to the lowest level of public esteem.

The implication is obvious. Only a few pastors remain bachelors, and fewer still experience overtly broken marriages. The expectation to be met, therefore, is that the marriage must remain apparently sound, and no family crisis must be allowed to surface. For large numbers of clergy couples, therefore, in the light of what we are now beginning to learn about them, the name of the game is "Let's Pretend." Whatever the reality, a surface appearance of harmony must be maintained. Otherwise, ecclesiastical superiors are going to be on edge, and colleagues are going to present the cold shoulder.

5. *Inner Compulsions of the Clergy Couple.*

The couples who responded to our studies clearly blamed congregational expectations for their discomforts.

But as often happens, they may in fact have been projecting on the congregation something that really came from their inner selves.

This raises some intriguing questions. Are pastors particular kinds of people who are driven by excessive needs to fulfill impossible demands? Certainly the ministry seems to have a special appeal to the idealist and the perfectionist. We have encountered some studies (Booth, Bowers, and Morentz, for example) that have hinted or suggested that pastors and their wives may in large measure consist of specific psychological types, and that understanding of their inner dynamics will explain their particular behavior patterns, and of course their marital interactions.

We have not found enough evidence to accept this hypothesis. We see a danger that those who counsel with ministers in trouble may judge the many in terms of the few. The ministry today is a broad-based profession, calling for a wide variety of motivations and skills, and therefore appealing to an equally wide variety of personality types.

However, there can be no doubt that the kinds of pressures we have examined in this chapter may well be producing in ministers and their wives, regardless of their personality patterns, strong compulsions to model very high standards of marital happiness and family felicity. Our final task in this chapter will be to explore this circumstance and try to determine whether, in fact, it is favorable or unfavorable to clergy marriages.

"Let your light so shine before men, that they may see your good works and give glory to your Father who is in heaven" (Matt. 5:16).

Surely no one will seriously question that this passage in the Sermon on the Mount applies to the quality of our family life. A central element in our Christian witness is that our faith should be demonstrated in the way we live together and relate to one another at home.

Surely, however, this is an injunction to *all* Christians, and *equally* to all Christians. Or is it? Have we any grounds for saying that a higher standard of family life is required of the man in the pulpit, and of his wife, than is required of the couples in the pews?

John Scanzoni, in his unpublished doctoral dissertation completed in 1964, examined this question very thoroughly. He discovered that ministers were deeply divided about it. One group, whom he called "sect clergy," took the view that they and their wives must accept higher standards than the couples in their congregations. The other group, whom he called "church clergy" (the terminology seems unfortunate) held that the same standards apply to both the clergy and the laity. Another difference between the two types was that the sect clergy believed that the minister's duties to the church must come before his duty to his family. The church clergy held that the minister was equally called to serve his church and his family.

Consider for a moment the image of the minister that is deliberately presented to the congregation. When the members gather for worship, he occupies the pulpit. Raised high above the congregation, and apart from all others, he is marked out as special, different, the authority. When he preaches, he is delivering the authentic Christian message. Sunday by Sunday, he tells the congregation how to live the Christian life. He has the answers. He is not "one of us"—he is set apart. The very posture required of the congregation, looking up to him from a lower level, emphasizes that he is the leader, the teacher, the guide.

The obvious implication is that, if he is the one to *tell* us how to live the Christian life, he should also be the one to *show* us. If, therefore, the congregation expects the pastor's family members to be models, has not the pastor himself, by accepting an exemplary and superior position, communicated this message to his people? Are they not responding to the clear signal he has given them?

Something else, too, must be considered. The pastor is not simply a leader, an authority. He also exercises priestly functions that are forbidden to all other members of the church. He administers the sacraments, receiving the power to do so from his ordination. In this capacity he acts directly as the representative of Christ, and this gives him a special aura of holiness. It was actually this factor—the special ministry of the altar—that led the Catholic Church in the first place to forbid marriage to its priests. The one who served as Christ's representative must be pure—and that meant, above all else, sexually pure.

So it seems that a minister can't have it both ways. By accepting the status of exemplar and priest, he inevitably implies his acceptance of a modeling role—as man, as husband, and as father.

When people in public office find that they cannot measure up to the idealized expectations of those whom they represent, they are often forced to conceal their shortcomings and build around themselves a system of defenses and pretenses. The result is that soon the outward appearance comes to be accepted as reality, and the only way to maintain status is by putting on an act.

We would suggest that this brings us to the heart of the complaint of so many clergy couples about the unreasonable expectations of their congregations. These couples are just too honest and sincere to be comfortable about putting on an act, and yet they feel exploited by the demands that seem to be placed upon them.

We think that these couples must have the courage to affirm their humanness. This inevitably involves some risks, because it means making themselves vulnerable. However, one of the exciting discoveries of the marriage enrichment movement is that it is precisely by giving up our pretenses, and being open and honest about where we really are, that we get through to other couples who have also been hiding behind defense systems. This is particularly true of couples in leadership roles. Indeed, in selecting couples for leadership training for marriage enrichment, one of the most important qualities we look for is a degree of emotional security that is sufficient to enable them, in order to develop trust in other couples who need their help, to make themselves vulnerable.

Some clergy couples have already had the courage to break through in this way, and we have never known such a couple to lose the respect of their church members. On the contrary, the response has been, "Thank God our pastor and his wife are being honest with us. Now we can be equally honest with them and with one another."

Being honest about our humanness is not an acknowledgment of failure in our marriages. It is, in fact, the very opposite. It is an admission of the simple truth that for any couple to achieve their full relational potential is a very difficult task, calling for long years of growth and change. It is only when a couple can openly admit this, and link up with other couples for mutual help and support in the growth process, that they are at last free to be the people they really are, and delivered from the need to pretend that they are something other than they are.

The central truth we must all sooner or later accept is the fact that there is no such thing as a *perfect* marriage. It is also doubtful whether any marriage can even be called *good* unless it is involved in a continual, ongoing process of growth. The traditional idea that marriage is static is simply not in accordance with the facts. And the outside appearance of stability in marriages provides us with no clear indication of how healthy or unhealthy the relationships are on the inside.

We, therefore, take the view that the main reason why many clergy couples so strongly resent having high congregational expectations imposed upon them is because this touches them at a very sensitive spot—the distressing and exasperating fact that they secretly cherish the same high expectations for themselves, but have not yet been able to realize them.

After all, is it not right and proper for Christians to set high standards for their marriages and family relationships? And wouldn't those clergy couples be happy and grateful if they were in fact living up to these high standards, and measuring up to the expectations of the congregation and of the community? Surely, then, the answer is for the couples concerned to acknowledge that, being human, they have not yet reached their goals; but that they are deeply committed to a continuing effort to do so, and that they invite couples who are church members to join them, and help and support them in their ongoing quest.

Let us conclude this chapter with a very practical suggestion. Here is something that we invite you, as a clergy couple, to do together.

Each of you should first, separately and without collaboration, make a list of any and all aspects of your family life in which you feel the congregation expects you to behave in an unrealistic way or to measure up to some unreasonable standard.

When this has been done, set aside at least an hour of uninterrupted time to sit down together and share your lists. Then divide these items into two categories:

1. Those in which your right to decide what is Christian is being overruled by other people. You feel deeply convinced that your behavior is justified, but you sense that your church members, or at least a majority of them, feel otherwise.

2. Those in which you yourselves feel challenged. You know you really ought to measure up, but the painful truth is that you are not as yet doing so. The expectations of the congregation, therefore, make you feel guilty and inadequate.

Now consider what action to take. Are you prepared to gather together a small, carefully selected group of married couples from the congregation, share all this with them honestly and openly, and ask for their help and support?

CHAPTER VI

The Tyranny of Time

Kathleen Nyberg says: "There is a quaint saying: 'The minister only works on Sunday.' . . . Numbers of people still think ministers loaf around the house, staying in bed until noon. They think a minister works on special occasions, such as weddings. And after all, a wedding takes only fifteen minutes and is fun!" (P.41). It is hard for anyone who knows the true facts to credit this gross misconception. In his foreword to Daniel Walker's book, *The Human Problems of the Minister*, Bishop Gerald Kennedy, who ought to know, sets the record straight: "The ministry is a hard job, and no man who expects to be less than the hardest-working man in his community ought to undertake it."

This issue comes up again and again in every investigation that is made on the special difficulties that occur in the clergy marriage. In addition to its frequent occurrence in our own studies, Denton (page 80) found that two out of three of all the ministers' wives in his research project raised it.

When we try to analyze the complaints about the pastor's heavy schedule, we find a number of components:

1. *The Pastor's Many Roles:*

Most occupations tend to be clearly defined. A job specification can be drawn up which describes certain responsibilities to be assumed and certain operations to be performed. There are clearly defined hours of work and usually a specific place where it is done.

The task of the ministry simply cannot be fitted into that kind of framework. In a much-quoted article in *The Christian Century* (April 25, 1956) Samuel W. Blizzard, who had made a study of 690 clergymen, stated that whatever the ministry was in the past, it is now a profession. Moreover, the roles have multiplied so rapidly that, unlike the doctor and the lawyer, who are trained to carry out certain clear and prescribed functions, the minister must develop a whole set of roles, including some for which he has had no training at all.

Blizzard listed the six major roles as follows:

(a) *Administrator.* The *supervision* of the activities in the local church and parish.
(b) *Organizer.* The *development of programs* in the church and community.
(c) *Pastor.* Caring for the needs of church members. This includes counseling.
(d) *Preacher.* Proclaiming the gospel.
(e) *Priest.* Performing religious functions, such as leading worship, conducting baptisms, weddings, and funerals.
(f) *Teacher.* Giving instruction in the Christian faith.

It appears from Blizzard's study that *parishioners often put most emphasis on the roles for which the pastor has been least trained* and which he himself regards as least important—administration and organization.

This represents the kind of dilemma that the minister has to face. With only so many hours available, to which of his many tasks will he devote his major attention? In *The New Testament Image of the Ministry* by W. T. Purkiser, Elton Trueblood has pointed out: "It is hard for [the minister], in the midst of competing and very contradictory pressures, to know who he is. This basic problem must be solved before lesser problems can be rightly stated. Is he prophet, teacher, promoter, performer, preacher, counselor, visitor, business manager, or what?"

In the same book Pierce Harris, a Methodist minister, expressed it even more vividly:

The modern preacher has to make as many visits as a country doctor, shake as many hands as a politician, prepare as many briefs as a lawyer, and see as many people as a specialist. He has to be as good an executive as the president of a university, as good a financier as a bank president; and in the midst of it all, he has to be so good a diplomat that he could umpire a baseball game between the Knights of Columbus and the Ku Klux Klan! (p. 19)

2. The Pastor's Heavy Workload.

Obviously a task of such broad and varied dimensions will consume a great deal of the pastor's time. Blizzard's study included an assessment of the actual number of hours ministers were at work. He found that the professional working day averaged just under ten hours (rural pastors nine and a quarter, urban pastors ten and a half), divided up as follows: as admistrator, 40 percent; as pastor 25 percent; as preacher and priest 20 percent; as organizer 10 percent; as teacher 5 percent. Notice that over half of his total time goes in administration and organization.

If we assume a seventy-hour week (Kathleen Nyberg has a chapter in her book entitled "The Eighty-Hour Week Made Easy"), what we are interested in knowing is how much of that time the minister is at home, and how much of what is left over is shared with his family? John G. Koehler investigated this in a study of 119 American Baptist ministers (*Pastoral Psychology*, September 1960). He asked their wives to keep careful records of the amount of waking hours the pastor spent at home in a given week. Here are the percentages for the ministers in each of five categories:

At home less than ten hours per week—6%
At home ten to nineteen hours per week—39%
At home twenty to thirty hours per week—30%
At home thirty to forty hours per week—18%
At home more than forty hours per week—7%

The mean was about twenty-six hours, or under four waking hours a day. This of course included meals at home; dressing, undressing, washing and shaving; household and family duties; reading and personal hobbies and pursuits; watching TV; in some cases, sermon preparation and entertaining parishioners and guests.

Koehler also investigated how much free time these ministers had. Less than half of the churches involved encouraged their pastors to take a day off. But even when they did, the pastors didn't generally avail themselves of it. During the four-week period in which the wife reported, only half of the husbands had taken any time off at all and only two of them had taken a regular day off each week.

3. Working When Others Are Free.

As everyone knows, Sunday is the pastor's busy day; Saturday is often sermon preparation time; and most of the important church meetings, and many counseling sessions, are scheduled in the evenings. These, of course, are the very times when the average worker is at liberty—the time when family events are generally scheduled. On weekdays, the children are at school, and if the pastor's wife has an outside job, she also will be otherwise engaged in the daytime. So the times that he might most conveniently set aside for family activities are the very times when this is least convenient for the other family members.

4. The Element of Uncertainty.

The Koehler study found that a major complaint of the wives was that pastors never know for sure when they can be at home. In our own investigation, the term "on call twenty-four hours a day" frequently occurred. Family activities that are planned ahead, then have to be canceled, produce a great deal of frustration and bitterness. One wife said, "If a woman with marriage problems keeps my husband at the church when I expected him home, I wonder whether my need of him may be greater than hers!"

5. *Much of the Work Is Emotionally Exhausting.*

While the variety of the pastor's job is welcomed by most, and it involves little dull routine, inevitably it brings a good deal of stress. This is due to two factors. First, the pastor often has to deal with human suffering and tragedy. He is the one who must offer cheer to the sick, support to the dying, comfort to the bereaved. He must step in and deal with poignant human crises that others prefer to avoid. In his counseling he must cope with all the negative emotions that surface in deeply troubled people.

He must also endure a good deal of frustration. Aware that more tasks confront him than he can ever carry out, he is always making difficult and painful choices. When things go wrong and he is in low spirits, he must contrive to appear cheerful and self-possessed. Often, by the time he finally gets home, his energy is drained by chronic fatigue, and he has little to offer to his waiting wife, who may also be on edge. Such situations can easily become explosive.

6. *His Sense of Vocation Makes Him Compulsive.*

When the going is hard and he feels ready to call it quits, he remembers that this is his sacred duty, and he must go on. This is his cross, and he must bear it patiently and with fortitude. So he may be tempted to "press on toward the mark" when it might really be better to stop and reassess the situation. This urge to drive himself produces ministers who, in the vivid term coined by Wayne Oates, become "workaholics"; who feel virtuous as long as they keep relentlessly going and unworthy if they stop for a break. As one wife expressed it, her husband developed a "guilty conscience" if he spent time relaxing at home.

It all adds up to a sad and serious situation. What can be done about it?

In our attempts to find solutions, we came back again and again to the fact that the pastor's heavy schedule is, very largely, of his own making. If this sounds like a judgment, it is offered only as a step toward a positive solution.

Any pastor whose marriage and family life are threatened by time pressure could profitably examine where he stands in three areas.

The first is *personal ambition*. The success syndrome, so pervasive in American culture, seems to operate with special intensity for the minister. He is on display before the public—in the pulpit, presiding over meetings, performing ritual functions—for a large part of his time. In the glare of the limelight, his performance is constantly being assessed. The ladder to higher and higher status is ever before him, and the competition is fierce. His self-esteem is closely related to his image in the eyes of those around him. Earning the praise of others helps suggest that a higher voice is also saying, "Well done, good and faithful servant."

However, the pastor needs to do some deep heart-searching about all this. Are his frantic efforts really furthering the Christian cause or bringing the kingdom of heaven nearer? Even if this is possible, is the gain justified if it is achieved by neglecting those who are nearest, and should be dearest, to him? Let no man say it is impossible to change. Koehler, in *Ministers' Wives* by William Douglas, cites one wife's story.

For the first seven years of our ministry my husband was "too busy" for regular days off. It was his physician who asked him if he were trying to save the world in the first ten years of his ministry and die or become disabled at an early age. . . . My husband took stock of himself and his job and made the decision. He works like a beaver six days a week . . . and plans the one day as a "date" with me or with the family. (p. 87)

Second, is the *order of his priorities*. The work of the minister, as we have seen, lacks clearly defined frontiers. He is not protected by office hours, or by the geographical separation of the work place and the home refuge. His task is not even confined to his church. The community and the denomination, not to mention free-lance, outside opportunities to speak and write, make claims on him that are often subtle and seductive. When the priorities are not

The Tyranny of Time

firmly assessed and established, there is a strong tendency
for marriage and the family to end up at the bottom of the
list. He had better decide that he will never be able to do all
that he ought to do, and (with his wife's help) establish
limits for himself that his job specification fails to provide.

The third area is *time management*. The pastor should
ask himself whether he is clearly *distinguishing between
quantity and quality*. Time is by itself an inaccurate and
misleading measure of accomplishment. Sometimes by
chance, but often as a result of careful management, a great
deal gets achieved within a short time span. On other
occasions, a great deal of time is spent in achieving nothing
at all.

This has special relevance to the marriage relationship.
A husband might yield to an importuning wife's demand
that he spend more evenings at home, and even promise to
do so; only to find that the relationship is much worse in
consequence. A short period of honest, daily sharing in–
depth between husband and wife, or five minutes of warm
mutual affirmation, is worth many hours of superficial
togetherness.

A minister of our acquaintance, when asked about his
wife, acknowledged that he had been so busy that he had
hardly seen her for several days. Rather glibly, he said, "We
just pass on the stairs." Even that brief contact could be
given quality if, on the stairs, he had paused to kiss or
embrace her, or simply to say, "I love you."

In this connection we might offer a word of counsel to the
frustrated wife of the "overworked" minister. She also may
not be handling the situation wisely.

A wife frustrated because her husband returns home so
late will not be likely to give him a warm welcome when he
does return. He may, in fact, have been caught in a difficult,
demanding situation, and may be himself frustrated about
returning so late. If he is accepted with sympathetic
understanding, and listened to, his wife can commiserate
with him, enable him to feel understood; and then she can,
without blaming or being judgmental, share with him how
lonely she felt in his absence, and how eagerly she had been
longing for his return.

If a husband does not seem eager to come home, or to plan time with his wife, she may have to ask why he does not put a high value on her company. Charles William Stewart speaks of "ministers who find themselves getting cool toward the spouse and retreating to the church study or using a busy schedule as an excuse to stay away. The drying up of affection between them and the neglect of their sexual life are symptomatic of the harried mate's use of business as a retreat from the marriage."

In such a situation the wife, at a carefully chosen time, might share her concern with her husband and ask him directly whether she is failing him in some way. This may raise some difficult issues, but it is much better to face them and work them through together, with help if necessary, than to let the relationship degenerate further still. This situation could, of course, happen the other way around, when the husband senses indifference in his wife.

It can safely be assumed that a married couple who love and cherish each other will actively desire to spend time together and will generally find ways of making this possible. The amount of time shared, and the quality of that time, will usually reflect the quality of the relationship.

Take heed, therefore, and beware. If you are not having enough time alone together, why? If it is because you don't seem to want or need it, there's something wrong with your marriage. Find out what it is and put it right.

Kathleen Nyberg says, "If there is a villian in the minister's story, his name is time. This villian can steal away a man's essential resources before he is mature enough to realize that he has been victimized." (p.22)

Let us conclude this chapter with some ideas and suggestions about how this villian can be exposed and defeated.

1. Time has become a tyrant for most of us because life is much more complex than it was in the past. Our outreach is almost incredibly extended. Through radio and TV we get information about events all over the world almost immediately after they have happened. We can be reached by telephone, in a matter of minutes, from distant cities and

even distant countries. The automobile and the airplane can take us to places that our forefathers would never have considered visiting. Opportunities for learning, for experiencing, for entertainment are available to us in such variety that our problem is to decide what to select and what to reject. We live amid what the French call an "embarrassment of riches." The time pressures that result might be called "the disadvantages of our advantages."

2. Time pressure has become a major item in recent years for married couples and for families. This is largely because most of us spend much more of our day out of our homes than ever before; and this applies to fathers, mothers, and children alike. Safeguarding time-alone-together has come to be a continual struggle for couples who want to develop and enjoy the resources of their relationship.

3. All this is specially true of clergy marriages. The multiple tasks of today's minister reflect the increased complexity of life generally; and in some special areas—particularly administration and counseling—very time-consuming new roles have been added to the traditional ones. Also, with more and more clergy wives being employed outside the home, new pressures have been introduced into the scheduling of family events.

4. Under these conditions, it is much more true than ever before that "your time is your life." The extended span of years that we enjoy today can actually be canceled out by the misuse and wasting of the passing hours. We need to heed the message of the son of Thomas Huxley, who was once asked how his father had managed to achieve so much in one lifetime. His reply was brief but challenging, "My father knew the difference between ten minutes and a quarter of an hour."

5. We need particularly to examine our addiction to the major time-wasters—TV, magazines and newspapers, and the telephone. People who have significant major goals in life are very disciplined about TV programs; but many others are not, and the weekly averages for watching-hours are quite appalling. Telephone conversations, also, are highly seductive. Try switching on a kitchen timer when

you lift the phone and pinning on the wall a list of effective ways to terminate politely a conversation that is getting nowhere.

These are general recommendations. Let us add a few more that may specially help a minister and his wife.

6. Learning to say no graciously. It is flattering to receive many invitations, but to accept them all can push more vital experiences out of our lives. One good rule is never to make a final decision on the telephone, but to say you will think it over and call back. This is specially important when both husband and wife are involved. In other situations, it is hard to know how to decline without seeming unappreciative. This art can be practiced by a couple together, and it is similar to terminating conversations in a manner that leaves the other person feeling affirmed and appreciated. A good line is, "I'm honored to be asked, and would love to come. But if I do, I would be letting someone else down and I'm sure you won't want me to do that!"

7. It's a good discipline to keep a time schedule for a typical week, accounting roughly for every quarter hour. This enables you to see how your days are spent and to readjust your priorities. It is especially helpful for husband and wife to do this separately and then go over the records together.

8. The pastor's weekly time schedule can be used to evaluate his various roles and functions in terms of their respective worth. The questions to ask are, Was this really necessary? and Is this kind of activity profitable enough to justify the time it takes? Unless such questions are raised periodically, church programs can go on automatically, which are no longer fulfilling any useful purpose. It is senseless for a burdened pastor to be overworked, and neglectful of his family, merely to turn a wheel with nothing being produced.

9. A very effective minister we knew made for himself a rule that he would never do himself anything that anyone else could do for him. At first this sounds as if he had an exaggerated idea of his own importance. But it really makes good sense. It enables him to spend his time on activities

for which he is uniquely qualified; and at the same time, it involves many other people, according to their gifts, in being part of the team that serves the church. The concept of the pastor as facilitator and supervisor is in fact a very creative one. By training laypersons to function effectively he is not only saving his time, but also promoting their growth. For example, we see no reason why a pastor should not pick a few talented and promising men and women and train them to preach, so that occasionally his time for sermon preparation could be cut back, freeing him for a relaxed and enjoyable Saturday with the family.

10. We are more and more convinced that the really effective way to deal with the minister's time problem is to work on a contract with the congregation. We are not at all of the opinion that church members want to work their ministers to death. So we suggest a contract for a specified number of hours per week—say fifty to sixty. One complete day off should be included—or a day and a half. This would mean about nine hours per working day. Of course, in one week it might go over this, but that could be balanced by extra free time later. A small committee of responsible laypersons could be appointed to meet with the minister and his wife, say once a month, to check up on his schedule and make sure that the needs of the church, of the family, and of the minister himself were being adequately and fairly met. If not, the contract could be adjusted accordingly. It seems to us that the tyranny of time for the clergy couple needs to be met head on in a practical and realistic fashion and that this would be the best way to do it. How about giving it a try?

CHAPTER VII

Parsonages and Moving Vans

When clergy couples list the disadvantages of their way of life, living conditions are frequently mentioned. The chief complaint is the glasshouse or fishbowl syndrome, which robs the family of privacy. In our study, 52 percent of the husbands and 38 percent of the wives specifically listed this. In addition, for a variety of other reasons, 11 percent of husbands and 16 percent of wives expressed dissatisfaction with housing arrangements.

The target of practically all of these attacks is the parsonage system. One wife summed it all up in these words:

The parsonage is a disadvantage. The couple misses out on sharing in their own home—the planning and decorating together; the financing, which helps them to understand money management; learning to take responsibility for maintaining their property; and having a sense of security for the future. Also, living next door to the church has been a source of stress for our family. Church people tend to invade our yard and take advantage of the small children.

We were puzzled about that reference to the children until we found, in a book on pastoral work by Andrew Blackwood published in 1945, a reference to "fools who kiss little girls on the cheek and pat little boys on the head" (p. 59). The parsonage system seems also to be closely related to the complaint that the family "belongs" to the congregation, mentioned by 9 percent of the husbands and 11 percent of the wives.

Some of the negative findings about the parsonage have found their expression in a wry form of humor. For example, Welthy Fisher in *Handbook for Ministers' Wives* coins this definition of a parsonage:

A professional annex . . . where all and sundry may drop in at any hour for an unscheduled chat or meal, where an emergency committee can meet, where more mail and telephone calls than any one can cope with will be received. . . . and where budgets are perennially stretched beyond the resiliency of even rubber! It is also a place where a family is raised, a personal home maintained, and the life of the mind and spirit set forward. (p. 16)

From the same source comes the quote from a minister's wife who said, "Our parsonage is the only house in town that is never locked, and the only one where people walk in and out without knocking."

Paul Martin, in a booklet entitled *Life in a Parsonage*, says there are two kinds of parsonages—those with "five rooms and a bath" and those with "three rooms and a path."

A story going the rounds describes a pastor's wife giving an order to a grocery clerk. She gives him the address for delivery, and he asks, "Is that a private house?" Her reply, "No, its a parsonage. It's as public as a hotel lobby, and people come and go all day, just as they do at the post office."

In a more serious vein Elizabeth Dodds, in an article on "The Minister's Homemaker" in *Pastoral Psychology*, December 1960, summarizes a series of letters she received from ministers' wives as follows: "The parsonage is an anachronism, an outdated source of pressure on ministers' families and of bickering between pastor and people."

In the light of such a barrage of criticism, we may well ask how the churches ever got to providing parsonages in the first place.

It is helpful to remember that in New Testament times there were no church buildings. Groups of Christians in a community would meet for worship in a private house. In Acts 12, for example, when Peter was delivered from prison and found himself in the streets of Jerusalem, he naturally made his way to the house of Mary, the mother of John Mark, confident that the local Christian community would be gathered there; as indeed they were. Paul's letters often include greetings to "the church that is in your house." All through the ages, missionaries have tended to arrange for groups of new converts to meet for worship and fellowship in private homes, until a suitable building could be erected.

In the late Middle Ages, it was customary to provide the priest with a house, usually close to the church where he ministered. The celibate priest often had a local woman or girl to live in as a housekeeper. After the Reformation, when Protestant ministers were allowed to marry, the housekeeper was replaced by a wife. In the Anglican churches in England, the home of the minister, usually called the vicarage or the rectory, was often a large and commodious building, for England's country parsons were distinguished for the size of their families. Samuel Wesley, for example, fathered nineteen children, including Charles and John, the founders of Methodism, and his rectory at Epworth had eighteen rooms. Susannah Wesley's father, Dr. Samuel Annesley, had a total of twenty-five children.

The English housing plan (the equivalent Scottish word is "manse") must have taken root in America in the early colonial period. Certainly the traditional practice of providing the minister and his family with a home that belonged to the church became almost universal over here. So the parsonage represents an ancient and honorable tradition. William Douglas speaks of the way in which

the physical care of a minister and his family by a congregation . . . takes on deep meaning. For it symbolizes a relationship which can be either mutually satisfying and rewarding or mutually frustrating and problematic. The parsonage and salary represent the caring relationship in which the congregation must learn how to care for others without dominance, and the minister and his family must learn to be cared for without dependence. . . . At its best, when a minister, his wife, and congregation share a common commitment and calling, the caring relationship expresses a covenant. (p. 184)

Kathleen Jarvis, in her book The Impressions of a Parson's Wife, wrote movingly in 1951 of the English rectory, built in 1846, where she lived.

Sometimes, when I pursue my daily round of household affairs . . . I find myself thinking of all the other people to whom this house was home.

74

Babies have been born, and people have died in these rooms; joy and sorrow have ruffled the even tenor of the grey house, as a stone thrown into a pond breaks the still surface of the water which eddies, ripples, and is still again. Heavy theological discussions and the light-hearted laughter of children have echoed within these walls. . . .

Shall we, too, have left our mark long after we have departed, when those yet unborn will think out their sermons in the study which overlooks the lawn, or stir the bubbling fruit in their preserving pans as the fragrance . . . fills the sunny kitchen? (pp.51-52)

But we live in a changing world. Today's pastor need no longer have his home next to the church, because he can be there in his automobile in a matter of minutes. Anyway, he can easily be reached by telephone. In modern communities the pace is often fast and furious, and the pastor needs a place in which he can find refuge from the daily pressures. The pastor's wife of today also wants a place she can call her own—a home she can furnish to suit her taste, and where she can be free of invasion by well-intentioned, but sometimes insensitive parishioners whose visits are not always welcomed, and who may treat the parsonage as an adjunct of the church.

Add to this the ravages of inflation, and the fact that real estate has become for most of us the best form of security for our future, and the case for a new approach to housing for the minister's family becomes totally convincing.

Change has in fact been taking place for some time. When Douglas made his study in the early 1960's, 78 percent of the clergy wives lived in unfurnished parsonages, 15 percent in furnished parsonages, and only 7 percent received a housing allowance. But when asked what their preference would be, twice as many as already had the housing allowance said they would favor that system. About the same time (1966) the General Assembly of the Presbyterian Church of the U.S.A. made this recommendation: "The healthful trend toward providing a household allowance rather than a subsidized dwelling has reduced one of the classical stresses on the minister's wife; namely, that of living in the 'social fishbowl.' " More recent trends may be judged from two sources. A survey of 183 pastors' wives, reported in 1976 by Kenneth Hayes of the Southern Baptist Convention, found that 62 percent lived in unfurnished parsonages and 19 percent owned their own homes and received a housing allowance. By way of contrast, a United Presbyterian study carried out by Mary Mattis, and reported in 1977, found that 49 percent of the clergy wives polled lived in houses owned by the family, while 45 percent lived in a home provided by the congregation. The differences in these figures may be explained by the fact that many Southern Baptist pastors have had minimal training, serve small congregations, and move frequently; whereas Presbyterian congregations are relatively larger and wealthier. So the difference between 19 percent and 49 percent in these two studies shows a wide range of clergy couples who receive a housing allowance. However, the direction of the overall trend seems to be clear. The Presbyterian finding was that home ownership is favored decidedly more often by the younger clergy wives than by the older ones.

Such a trend, if inflation continues at anything like the present rates, may become irreversible. Few churches would wish to sell a parsonage and then have to buy another a few years later at a greatly increased price.

If you are a clergy couple who will continue to live in parsonages, a few words of comfort may be in order.

- Many of the tall tales will not bear investigation. For example, Denton found among the wives he interviewed only one whose parsonage door had ever been opened without knocking, and the intruder was an elderly lady, senile and confused.

- The loss of privacy doesn't bother some clergy families. "You get used to it," said one wife. Another said, "You get to be like a goldfish yourself—you don't really care." Yet another pointed out that the people who look into the glasshouse are also the people who hasten to your aid when you are in trouble.

- Several writers point out that invasion of the parsonage is often unconsciously encouraged when the pastor and his wife adopt an open-door policy that then gets out of hand. It is possible, without being rude, to communicate the message that this is a family home, and that privacy is valued.

- For those who have some choice about the parsonage they will occupy, the evidence suggests that privacy is more often respected in a city church than in a rural one; that the further from the church the parsonage is located, the fewer visitors appear; that a large, spacious parsonage has some decided advantages in providing places to which one can retreat and where children can play; but, of course, the heating bills will be higher.

- For those who are consulted about *building* a new parsonage, Lora Lee Parrott's book *How to Be a Preacher's Wife and Like it* actually includes a description of "My Dream Parsonage."

Moving Vans

In our study, 14 percent of husbands and 13 percent of wives complained about the "itinerant system" that uproots clergy families from time to time by moving them to new churches.

To get this in perspective, we need to remember that in the U.S. population as a whole one family in five makes a household move every year. In California, where the population is almost nomadic, the frequency is decidedly higher than that. The situation is worse in the armed services. We once had lunch with an admiral of the navy who told us that his family had changed homes thirty-seven times in his thirty-five years of service.

Some people *like* moves—others emphatically do not. One wife, listing the disadvantages of the clergy marriage as she had experienced it, made her point clear by writing,

"Moving, moving, moving, moving, moving." We were told of another wife who said, "For me, hell is a moving van at the door."

The Methodists get the reputation of subjecting their ministers to frequent moves. Their connectional system has the power to allocate ministers to churches. In Britain the tradition was for a family to be moved every three years, unless there was a special reason not to do so. But for some time now the Methodist system, both in Britain and in the U.S.A., has been getting more flexible. Oddly enough, our inquiries suggest that the most moves are made by Southern Baptist pastors, where the average duration of service to a church is less than two years! This is explained in terms of the large numbers of part-time pastors, with little theological training, who service small rural congregations. The meager supply of sermons soon runs out!

The chief complaints about moving are that it involves a major upheaval, followed by the need to make a whole series of readjustments. For children particularly, it disrupts their education and separates them from their relatives in the extended family and forces them to live among strangers. Others say that it makes them wanderers on the face of the earth, without permanent roots.

There are, however, good reasons, both for pastors and congregations, why moving should be a possibility. In the Anglican Church in England, where a parson could secure a living and settle there for a lifetime, a parish with an unsuitable clergyman really suffered. A story is told about one such parish where the pastor was at last leaving. The grateful congregation planned a farewell party and decided to present him with a traveling case. A layman to whom this task was entrusted was illiterate and in his speech declared that "Mr. Smith has been our encumbrance here for thirty years; and now that he is leaving us, we have decided to give him a little momentum!"

Perhaps the increasing cost of moving, together with the new trend toward home ownership, will cut down in the future the frequency with which the moving van will appear at the door of the clergy family's home.

Finally, here is an exercise for you to do as a clergy couple, by way of examining where you are about your own present living arrangements.

Separately and without collaboration, use pencil and paper to ask and answer the following questions:

1. Given a free choice, in what order would you select these three possible housing options? ( ) furnished parsonage, ( ) unfurnished parsonage, ( ) housing allowance.

2. If your selection doesn't represent your present housing arrangement, how do you feel about it? ( ) very frustrated, ( ) somewhat frustrated, ( ) I can accept it without frustration.

3. Are there any aspects of your present housing situation that bother you? If so, make a list of them . . .

4. Do you have some practical suggestions to offer that could make your present housing situation better for all concerned? If so, make a list of them . . .

When you have finished the exercise individually, sit down together, share your responses, and talk about possible future action.

CHAPTER VIII

The Battle of the Budget

Just over one-third of the couples in our study (34 percent of husbands and 36 percent of wives) complained of financial stress—particularly when this compelled the wife to seek an outside job in order to balance the family budget.

To write anything about salaries and expenses at this time, with inflation rates fluctuating, is to run the risk that the statement may be out of date soon after the ink is dry. Here are some facts that will demonstrate our dilemma:

- When Harry Emerson Fosdick began his distinguished ministry at Riverside Church in New York City in 1924, his salary was five thousand dollars a year. He did not wish for more. He had some extra income from teaching, and he insisted that five thousand dollars was enough to enable him and his wife to live comfortably.

- The Reader's Digest of May 1959 reported a recent national survey which found that the average annual salary for ministers was $4,436 or $85.30 per week. For a sixty-hour week, that was just over a dollar and a half an hour!

- A report of the National Council of Churches of Christ in the U.S.A.(Professional Church Leadership) stated in 1973 that the median salary (from all sources) of American Protestant ministers was then $10,348. Fourteen percent of them received less than six thousand dollars, and 11 percent received more than sixteen thousand dollars.

What do all these figures tell us?

Not much, when we have experienced high rates of

inflation, with prices steadily going up and spending power steadily going down. It almost seems better for us to try to discuss clergy finances without using figures.

In the fourteenth century, Geoffrey Chaucer wrote his *Canterbury Tales*, and one of the pilgrims he described was the "clerk of Oxenford." In the original, his description would be almost unintelligible, so we have ventured to translate it roughly into modern English:

> There also came an Oxford clergyman,
> Well educated, specially in logic.
> His horse was as lean as a rake,
> And he himself was gaunt and slender.
> His coat was in rags and tatters;
> For although he was a philosopher
> His supply of money was meager.
> All that he could beg from his friends
> Was spent on books and learning;
> And he rewarded them by praying earnestly
> For the welfare of their souls.

Here we have the traditional prototype of the English clergyman. Poorly endowed with this world's goods, he has sought instead to enrich his mind and to build up treasure in heaven.

Closer to our own time, but still a hundred years ago, we have a fascinating account of an American clergy family. It is given in the foreword of *My Boyhood in a Parsonage*, written by Thomas W. Lamont, who succeeded J. P. Morgan as chairman of the Morgan Bank in New York City in 1943. He describes his early life as the son of a Methodist minister who, although he was a Hebrew, Greek, and Latin scholar, served a series of country parishes on the banks of the Hudson River during the final quarter of the nineteenth century. Here is the picture of their family life:

With clergymen's salaries in the country as low as they were when I was a boy, our household had to economize to an almost painful, and at times certainly ludicrous, degree. But that practice, perhaps becoming almost habit, probably did us no harm in its bearing on our later and more abundant years. We were reared with the simple idea that any possible spare income was to be given away freely but was never to be wasted. (p.27)

The reader must remember that in the world of which I speak we had no motorcars or buses, no telephones, no radio. Our houses were lighted by kerosene lamps, or at best by gas. A few of the larger cities had street horse cars, but no electric or trolley cars, and the kitchen and household gadgets for economizing labor that are a commonplace with us today were totally lacking.

When the couples in our study talk about "financial stress," what do they mean?

Not, obviously, anything like the kind of ascetic living standard of the Oxford clergyman, or of the clergy family in which Thomas W. Lamont grew up. And not the kind of tight budget on which the Spences had to manage in Iowa. Not even, we presume, the equivalent of the 14 percent of clergy families who in 1973 had to manage on less than six thousand dollars a year. We would imagine that all the couples we worked with were better off than that. Nevertheless, one-third of them felt that they were struggling with financial difficulties.

We may all rejoice that the extreme hardships of the past, which were so often borne with Christian fortitude, are no longer required of the vast majority of clergy families today. Where, however, do we set the upper limit?

Lucille Lavender champions with compaigning zeal the minister's right to be better paid. Writing in 1976, she quotes a report from the Bureau of Labor Statistics, U.S. Department of Labor, which presented a list of occupations, median annual earnings, and educational backgrounds. The lists were numbered, beginning with the highest paid occupation, and continuing on to the lowest paid. Out of 432 occupations listed, clergymen are number 316. They rank with the lowest paying occupations, such as farm laborers, waiters and waitresses, and cooks. Lucille Lavender comments:

"Though they rank next to the bottom economically, educationally they rank with the ten top earning occupations. . . . Most of those below their earning rank did not graduate from high school, while many did not go beyond the eighth grade. What is more disturbing is that the clergy showed the lowest percentage of salary increase among their professional peers in a ten-year period. (pp.63-74)

What is being argued here is that pastors should be ranked as professionals and paid accordingly.

A study made in 1973 by the National Council of Churches (Professional Church Leadership) probed the attitudes of 4,635 ministers throughout the United States using questionnaires that they completed. Ninety-three percent of them signified agreement with the question— "Overall, I am very satisfied with being in the ministry," and 83 percent of them were satisfied with their present congregations. When asked to respond to the statement "Years of working at a low salary have left me discouraged with the ministry," 84 percent did not agree. Even when confronted with the fact that their salaries are low, they were not deeply discouraged by this fact. In our own studies, two-thirds of both husbands and wives (in almost equal numbers) did not list financial stress as a significant disadvantage; and for those who did, the necessity for the wife to take a job to help out was a frequent emphasis.

Ministers on the whole, therefore, are not deeply concerned about their pay. This doesn't mean, however, that they wouldn't like it to be higher. In the National Council of Churches study, four out of five ministers thought they were underpaid compared with equally educated professionals (a fact eloquently demonstrated by Lucille Lavender); and two out of three felt that their salary was too low to meet their current family needs.

The picture that emerges is that ministers in general are strongly service-oriented, aware that they are relatively poorly paid, but willing to accept hardship and make sacrifices for the cause to which they have devoted their lives.

What if it were otherwise? We have seen teachers close down school systems, police leave criminals with a free hand, and fireman refuse to fight fires, in their strident demands for more pay. It would indeed be a sad sight if Christian ministers ever adopted such tactics.

If they did, could pastors be better paid? That obviously

depends mainly on the size of the congregation they serve. However, Lucille Lavender firmly insists that even congregations whose members earn only median incomes could pay their ministers much better salaries, if all the members tithed. We leave that suggestion for your consideration.

Clergy families that cannot manage financially have two major alternative sources of income. About 22 percent of the ministers in the N.C.C. study were pastoring several churches or had taken additional secular jobs. But for most families, extra income represents the earnings of clergy wives. About half of the wives of pastors in the N.C.C. study were working outside the home, and for more than half of these the principal reason stated was to augment the family income.

There are also, of course, some subsidiary gains that help clergy families. One is discounts in the stores and free professional services from community practitioners. Another is generous gifts, in cash or in kind, from members of the congregation. Kathleen Nyberg has a whole chapter about this, entitled "A Chicken for the Sabbath Pot." Some pastors' wives, however, find these "extras" embarrassing and humiliating; they dislike being the recipients of charity.

The financial difficulties of the clergy couple have produced their quota of sly humor. One minister is reported to have said that he didn't have any money worries, because he didn't have enough money to worry about! Another was described as having no time to spend looking for the lost sheep, because he was too fully occupied with his search for the lost coin. A third was asked by a pollster, "If you had to take a 10 percent reduction in your salary, where would you make the first cut?" He replied "Across my throat."

Welthy Fisher probably wraps it up when she says:

> Harsh as it may sound to put it bluntly, I believe it to be true that too often we attribute to the budget, difficulties which arise from our rejection of the job itself. You may raise a cynical eyebrow at this statement, but I would hazard a guess that there are no basic

problems of being a minister's wife which will be solved merely
by an increase in the budget. (pp.20-21)

Now, what about an exercise on your financial situation?
Here are some questions to ask and answer. Use the same
procedure as before. Complete the responses separately in
writing first, then get together for sharing, and finally arrive
at some decisions for action.

1. How do you feel about your present income? ( ) it is
very inadequate, ( ) our budget is tight, but not seriously
so, ( ) it is acceptable but only just, ( ) it is quite adequate
for our needs.

2. How well do you cooperate with each other in
managing your money? ( ) not at all well—it is a source of
tension in our relationship, ( ) not as well as we could, but
it isn't a major issue for us, ( ) we seem to manage
satisfactorily.

3. Are there aspects of money management that you
really need to work on together? If so, make a list of
them . . .

Now get together, exchange what you have written, and
give the financial side of your shared life a checkup.

PART III

Personal and
Interpersonal Aspects—The
View from Inside

CHAPTER IX

Marriage as Vocation

In this section of the book the focus will be on yourselves, as individuals and as a couple. However favorable the outside conditions of a particular parish appointment may be, if your relationship with each other is not based on a shared sense of purpose and direction, you will be in trouble. On the other hand, if you are truly united, deeply committed to sharing your lives and working as a team, then it is highly unlikely that any outside pressure will be able to divide you or defeat you.

In the next three chapters, therefore, we will examine the quality of your interpersonal relationship. For a clergy couple, this will depend on having a mutually shared sense of vocation. We believe, in fact, that this should be the foundation stone of *any* Christian marriage.

"As Jesus walked along the shore of Lake Galilee, he saw two brothers who were fishermen, Simon (called Peter) and his brother Andrew, catching fish in the Lake with a net. Jesus said to them, 'Come with me, and I will teach you to catch men.' At once they left their nets and went with him" (Matt. 4:18-20 TEV). This brief, yet dramatic, account marks the beginning of the Christian ministry. The two brothers had until now followed what could be considered a useful form of work—providing food for hungry people. But now they had set it aside to follow another vocation. Their response is so immediate that it might seem as if they had never considered such a change before. Obviously, however, they had been prepared for it. They had heard, or heard about, the preaching of John the Baptist, and perhaps of Jesus too. The call clearly came at a moment when they were ready to respond.

There are other stories like this in the Bible: The divine

Voice in the temple that called the child Samuel three times in the night (I Samuel 3); the revelation that came to Elijah in the cave on Mount Horeb (I Kings 19:9-18); and the blinding light on the Damascus road that changed the life of Paul (Acts 9: 3-9). Other men and women, at other times, have attributed their call to Christian service to vivid experiences of a similar character.

The great majority of ministers, however, would have to say that their call was an inward experience, following much thought and prayer, and accepted only after periods of doubt and uncertainty. It was a final coming together of a complex series of events that seemed to point more and more clearly in the same direction. An example of this in the New Testament is John 21: 15-17, in which Jesus said to Peter in effect, "If you have truly come to love me, demonstrate your love by taking care of my followers."

Behind the concept of a call to the ministry lies the belief that God has a purpose for the world that is being gradually worked out, not by cataclysmic acts of divine power, but through the devoted service of men and women who are ready to take up the specific tasks that are presented to them. The implication is that God is aware of what is going on and is using those who are dedicated to doing his will to put the pieces gradually together.

Responding to God's call is an act of faith. We are seldom presented with the kind of evidence of God's working that would be convincing testimony to our five senses. The case for God's intervention in the world, and even the case for his existence, are not established by scientific evidence. This may be a necessary condition to test our faith, and we must accept it as such. But the fact remains that, in the vivid words of Studdert-Kennedy, a much admired English chaplain in World War I, living the Christian life is "betting your life that God is good."

The question we want to raise, in relation to the clergy marriage, is this, If God calls men (and women) to devote their lives to the ministry, does he also call people to other tasks? The answer would seem to be clear so far as direct service to the Church is concerned. Through the ages, there have been "lower orders" for men who were not ordained

89

and for women who could not be ordained. Surely they also could claim to have been called to the tasks they performed. And in later times there have been missionaries—teachers, doctors, nurses, and others—whose service was surely as greatly valued as that of the preachers and who were fully members of the team. Indeed, Paul says; "There are different kinds of spiritual gifts, but the same Spirit gives them. There are different ways of serving, but the same Lord is served" (I Cor. 12:4-5 TEV).

Today we use the word "vocation" in a much wider sense than its root meaning of a religious call. Our dictionary defines it as "a regular occupation or profession, especially one for which one is specially suited or qualified." The underlying concept of service is however usually retained—an occupation engaged in primarily to make money, or to develop a product that doesn't elevate other people's lives, is not normally considered to be a vocation.

Now, after this digression, let us come to the point. If God calls a man to minister to the members of a congregation, could he not equally call a man and woman to minister to each other, and to the children born to them, in a Christian family? The function of the ministry is to care for and support those in need and to enable them in all possible ways to live the Christian life. Can that not be practiced as effectively in a home as in a church? Indeed, more effectively, because the depth and closeness of relationships in a church fellowship can seldom match those that are possible in a family.

Of course, it could be argued that the minister is "set apart" by his ordination in a special way, through a solemn religious ceremony. But are not the married couple also "set apart" from others in what for them, if they are sincere Christians, is an equally solemn religious ceremony?

At this point, we need to bring ourselves directly into the discussion. When we were married, one of us (guess which!) was a minister, and the other was qualified in what would be called a secular profession. We both believed, however, that our marriage was our response to a divine call. We even declared this, at our wedding reception, to

90

those who had attended the ceremony. We have never doubted this sense of vocation, and it has been a source of powerful motivation for us when we have had to struggle with difficulties that have arisen in our relationship.

However, as the years passed, another sense of vocation developed for us, which we interpreted as a further unfolding of the purpose that had originally brought us together. We felt that we were called to devote our lives to making marriages and families more loving and creative, beginning with our own. Unfortunately, the church served by the one who was a minister could not at that time accept this as a valid extension of Christian ministry, so the only course was to resign in order to respond to what was increasingly felt to be a more urgent call. Some years later we felt constrained to join the Society of Friends, a Quaker group that does not ordain ministers. So, in our particular case, the vocation to our marriage proved to be deeper and more enduring than the vocation to the ministry.

Admittedly this is an unusual situation, but it raises what we feel are some important questions for clergy marriages.

Temple Gairdner was a clergyman who spent his life as a missionary to Egypt. He had a very definite sense of marriage as a vocation. At the time when he made his proposal of marriage to Margaret Mitchell, she was in Scotland and he in Egypt, so it had to be done by mail. After receiving her reply, he wrote her a letter that has been preserved:

Your letter arrived this afternoon; I got it at 5:00 o'clock, put it unopened in my pocket, and rode out into the country. I felt I must read it alone and with God . . . . In the quiet light of the setting sun, I broke the seal and saw the YES. I bowed my head and took you from the hands of God; then gave yourself and myself back to Him to fulfill His utter will. . . . Please God these things will make something heavenly, something spiritual and ethereal in our relations one to another. Something that God may have pleasure in and use to His own glory." (p. 92)

As the time of the marriage approached, Gairdner observed what he called a "vigil" to prepare himself. Recorded in his diary at that time is a prayer:

That I may come near to her, draw me nearer to Thee than to her; that I may know her, make me to know Thee more than her; that I may love her with the perfect love of a perfectly whole heart, cause me to love Thee more than her and most of all. That nothing may be between me and her, be Thou between us, every moment. That we may be constantly together, draw us into separate loneliness with Thyself. And when we meet breast to breast, My God, let it be on Thine own. Amen. Amen.

No doubt there have been plenty of other clergy couples who experienced the same profound sense of God's calling in their coming together as husband and wife. We do not talk freely and openly of these deeply intimate experiences. But the question we are raising is whether the churches, at a time when marriage is being widely secularized, are losing the sense that for Christians it is a vocation; and if so, whether the call of the pastor and his wife to bear witness to all that a Christian marriage can mean is not as central in importance, at this time in history, as his call to serve a church. To put it more directly, may those high expectations of the people in the congregation be expressing a longing to see the true meaning of Christian love, as expressed in the relationship of a man and a woman "called" into the "holy estate" of marriage, proclaimed and demonstrated? Is it therefore possible that, at this particular time in history, there is no more powerful way in which a minister can preach the gospel than in the witness that he and his wife offer through their marriage?

If we have made our point clear about marriage as a vocation, we need to take the matter a stage further. We see the clergy couple as representing two clear and distinct, though related, callings—he to the work of the ministry, and both of them together to the witness they can offer through their marriage. The question that now arises is, How exactly is the vocation of the clergy *wife* defined?

The traditional idea was that her vocation was to care for and support her husband in every way possible, but to keep herself modestly in the background. She was essentially an enabler, providing her minister husband with the "creature comforts" he needed in order to go forth and fulfill his sacred tasks; and bearing and raising their children. These domestic duties have been considered a vocation of a sort, but on a much lower plane than the exalted level on which her husband functioned. Women were expected—and conditioned—to live on an *auxiliary* level and to ask for no more than that. Even in law, until relatively recently, a wife was considered to be a kind of shadow of her husband—a mere appendage of his personhood. So to speak of his vocation and hers in the same breath might have been awkwardly inappropriate, if not irreverent.

In very recent years, however, women have rebelled against this denial of their full personhood. Many Christian women have joined in this revolt. Some men have supported them, some have not. The issue has become confused because of the excessive and aggressive manner in which the demands of extremist sections of the Women's Liberation Movement have been made. But change is in the air, and in almost every walk of life today the victory of the movement for the full recognition of woman's personhood is being steadily won.

What this means is that, in finding and fulfilling your Christian vocation as a married couple, the wife's "call" and the husband's "call" must be given equal weight and importance. Surely God speaks to men and women equally. In Galatians 3:28 Paul said plainly, "There is no difference between . . . men and women; you are all one in union with Christ Jesus" (TEV). So whatever may be true of differences in social or professional status, in God's sight the task he gives to the husband and the task he gives to the wife must both be fully and equally recognized.

So let us look directly at your vocations. For the husband, there are two. By reason of his ordination he is called to minister to a congregation or to render some other specialized service to the church. By reason of his marriage vows he is called to minister to his wife and children. If at any given point these two vocations seem to clash, he must decide which should have the priority. The Scanzoni study has shown that ministers don't all agree about this. But the Protestant denominations generally seem to take the view that the minister should *equally* serve both. Nolan Harmon, in his book on ministerial ethics, says plainly, "A minister's relationship to his family is as high and as sacred as that to his Church." And an official statement quoted by him has been prepared by the Christian Church (Disciples of Christ) asking the pastor to make the following declaration, "I will be fair to my family, and will endeavor to give them the time and consideration to which they are entitled."

For the clergy wife, the situation is more complicated. Her basic vocation is to her family, and the marriage vow is in all respects as valid, and as binding, for her as for her husband. It is of course a joint vocation, in which they both share as equals, and to fulfill it faithfully they must both be in full agreement.

However, the wife can have two other vocations—one to the church, which is jointly shared with her husband; the other to a separate occupation or profession of her own. Let us look at each of these.

We have already discussed the issue of what a clergy wife is *expected* to do in the church. The opinions of 462 United Presbyterian pastors' wives on this subject were obtained and analyzed in the Mattis study. Eighty-eight percent of them agreed that the wife should be a *member* of her husband's congregation; 56 percent agreed that she should be very active in that church; 27 percent that she should be willing to assist in counseling; 26 percent that she should be willing to undertake a leadership role; and 15 percent that she should help with secretarial work or be available to deal with church telephone calls.

This study was completed in 1977, so it represents quite recent attitudes. What it shows is that modern clergy wives do not feel that they are under any binding obligations about *how* they help in the church. Nearly half of them do not feel they have to be very active, and three-quarters feel no desire to undertake a leadership role.

These opinions seem to be saying what we emphasized in our earlier discussion—that the wife can determine her degree of involvement in the congregation according to her own sense of vocation and her time priorities. The terminology used in the Mattis study is that she shall have the right to serve the church as a member "without special obligations or privileges."

We would however feel that, whatever else she does or does not do, the wife's sharing in her husband's ministry should involve *full support* for what he is doing; provided that he on his part fulfills the above-mentioned Disciples' Code by being "fair" to his family. The amount of the wife's *practical involvement* in her husband's work would be secondary. She might at times, while giving him full support, be unable to provide any practical help at all.

The final question is the wife's separate vocation. Increasingly, clergy wives are taking outside jobs. The percentage is actually higher than that for *all* wives—the reason usually given being that more and more clergy wives are now getting advanced education and qualifying for prestigious positions in the job market.

Obviously, a wife with a full-time responsible outside job, and her domestic duties in addition, will have little time left for taking on projects in the church—unless, of course, her job is church-related. So what will matter most is that her husband, who may have to help out with some of the household chores, knows that in his work he has her full support, as she has his in hers.

This raises another issue. The National Council of Churches study of pastors' incomes found that only about half of the wives with outside jobs worked primarily to meet the families' financial needs. The others apparently saw their occupations as being in some sense vocations. Indeed, in these days some pastors' wives are themselves pastors. So the wife of the minister *could* have not two vocations, but three—her home, her church, and her occupation!

What we have here is a very flexible situation in which the only constant is the full-time task through which the husband fulfills his ministry. Beyond that, the time he gives to home duties, and the time his wife gives to the family, her job, and the church will vary flexibly with the age of the children, the need for the wife to do outside work, and the practicability of her helping in the church. Working all this out in practice will call for high levels of

95

cooperation and teamwork. In other words, clergy couples have to manage a pretty complex situation, which requires of each of them a clearly defined and mutually accepted sense of vocation.

We offer an exercise for you to do together, as a step toward clarifying your attitudes to your own and each other's vocations. It would be wise to set aside a stretch of several hours for a full exploration of this, unless you feel that you have already discussed it together thoroughly.

Here are some questions to be answered, separately in writing first, then discussed together. Wherever possible, you should each record your own attitude and what you think is your partner's attitude.

1. Does the husband view his calling to serve the church as ( ) superior? ( ) equal to his calling to serve his family? What is the wife's view? ( ) superior? ( ) equal?

2. Does the wife recognize that her marriage to a minister involves her in a vocation to support him fully in his work? ( ) yes ( ) no. Does she further accept a vocation to ( ) be a member of the church? ( ) take an active part in church life as far as her time allows? ( ) assume a leadership role? ( ) help with letters and phone calls?

3. Does the wife feel that she is justified in taking an outside job? ( ) full-time? ( ) part-time? Does she now have such a job? ( ) yes ( ) no. If yes, is the arrangement satisfactory to her? ( ) yes ( ) no. Is it satisfactory to the husband? ( ) yes ( ) no.

4. Does the husband accept a share of the household chores as part of his vocaton to serve his family? ( ) yes ( ) no. Is the wife satisfied with the amount of household help he is willing to undertake? ( ) yes ( ) no.

5. Do you feel that you are both in full agreement in recognizing each other's vocations and the obligations they impose on you? ( ) yes ( ) no. If not, are you prepared to give time to discuss this fully until you can reach agreement? ( ) yes ( ) no.

CHAPTER X

What Makes a Marriage Christian?

> How beautiful, then the marriage of two Christians,
> two who are one in home, one in desire, one in the way of life they
> follow, one in the religion they practice. . . . Nothing divides
> them, either in flesh or in spirit. . . . They pray together, they
> worship together, they fast together; instructing one another,
> encouraging one another, strengthening one another. Side by side
> they visit God's church and partake of God's Banquet; side by side
> they face difficulties and persecution, share their consolations.
> They have no secrets from one another; they never shun each
> other's company; they never bring sorrow to each other's hearts.
> Unembarrassed they visit the sick and assist the needy. . . . see-
> ing this, Christ rejoices. To such as these He gives His peace.
> Where there are two together, there also He is present.

Believe it or not, these words were written by Tertullian,
a leader of the Church in the second century A.D. They
reflect a highly idealized image of the relationship between
the Christian husband and wife, in the setting of a shared
ministry.

In the last chapter we looked at your various vocations
and how they could be integrated with each other. In
particular, we looked at your vocation to a Christian
marriage. In this chapter we shall explore what we mean by
a Christian marriage. Let Tertullian, with his vivid picture
of the Christian ideal in the early Church, provide us with
our text.

Marriage is a very ancient institution. Edward Wester-
marck, whose pioneering studies were reported in his
three-volume *History of Human Marriage*, first published
in 1891, reached the conclusion that marriage, in one form
or another, has existed in all settled human communities in
the world, and for as far back as recorded history extends.

Of course, he interpreted marriage in very broad terms.
The first thing we have to say about Christian marriage is

that it sets certain clear conditions for the husband and wife to meet. These conditions are intended to make sure, as far as possible, that the *purposes* of Christian marriage will be fulfilled. There are three of these purposes, and they are found in most of the wedding rituals of the various churches. *The first purpose* normally listed is that marriage exists to insure that children, who are needed to replenish the earth and to continue the act of creation that God began, may be born into a social unit that will care for them in their helpless years, and bring them to maturity "in the nurture and admonition of the Lord."

The second purpose is to insure that the sex drive, implanted by God, will be directed aright, as an expression of caring and continuing love.

The third purpose is to provide companionship to a close and nurturing relationship, because God saw that "it is not good that the man should be alone" (Gen. 2:18a).

The Church has judged that these three purposes of marriage will be properly fulfilled only if three requirements are met.

The first requirement is monogamy—marriage between one man and one woman only. In many human cultures, especially in Africa, a man may have several wives; and in a few a woman may have several husbands. In the Old Testament, as we know, polygamy was often practiced. But the Christian rule has always been one man and one wife. If you look again at the picture Tertullian portrays, you will at once realize that a relationship so close and intimate could be maintained only between two people. The unit of Christian marriage is therefore what we call the "dyad."

The second requirement is fidelity, referring to the sex relationship. Because sex can easily get out of control (and there was plenty of evidence of this in the Roman Empire when Christianity began) the Christian community made the rule that sex was only right in God's sight when it was confined to the marriage partners.

The third requirement is commitment; Christians who marry commit themselves to each other for life. For centuries this meant no divorce at all for Christian couples, and the Roman Catholic Church still stands by this principle. Protestants, however, following Luther, have recognized that a marriage may be terminated in conditions of extreme hardship, and the partners permitted to remarry. But the churches try not to allow this permissive attitude to be abused.

The conditions of life today have changed a great deal since Tertullian's time. Yet these three objectives still hold; and the three requirements are still, with a little flexibility here and there, accepted as needful safeguards.

In attempting to define what makes a marriage Christian, we are confronted with another issue that has led to some disagreement.

As we all know, great changes are taking place in our culture today. One of these is the emergence of a new pattern for modern marriage. Sociologists see the husband-wife relationship as moving progressively from the traditional concept, which made it a hierarchical institution, to the new concept that sees it as a companionship relationship. This transition has created a difficult situation for some Christian couples, because the new pattern seems to be in conflict with a traditional view that the husband is the "head" of the wife—that his role is one of authority and hers of submission.

We will comment only briefly on this difference of opinion that exists about Christian marriage. First, it should be understood that the hierarchical view of marriage is in no sense distinctively Christian. It has been universal among all the major human civilizations—including the Hebrew tradition. It has the great advantage of keeping marriage stable by making it a one-vote system. It reflected the patterns of the societies in which it existed. All were structured hierarchically and continued to be so until the advent of democracy, which by giving all adults the right to vote introduced a revolution of gigantic proportions. The coming of the companionship marriage is a direct reflection of the democratic ideal, making it, for the first time, a two-vote system, with all the complications that inevitably result. To say that the companionship marriage is unchristian, therefore, would be another way of saying that democracy is unchristian. This may be the sincere view of some people, and in a democracy, of course, their right to say so will be fully respected.

The position we take here is that Christian tradition has defined its basic standards for marriage, which we have already outlined; and that as long as these are honored, the particular way in which the couple choose to relate to each other—a one-vote or two-vote system—is for them to decide. John Howell's recent book, *Equality and Submission in Marriage*, has very ably and thoroughly explored the biblical and theological issues involved and has traced a continuum from the rigidly hierarchical pattern of marriage to the flexible companionship model, with the possibility of many variations along the line. All, he asserts, are options for the Christian couple. We would agree.

It is interesting to notice that, in the description by Tertullian of a Christian marriage, the couple are equal companions in every respect. This was written little more than a hundred years later than the latest book in the New Testament.

So far we have been talking about the standards and values that define a Christian marriage. It is certainly necessary to have some understanding of these matters, but we would like now to return to more contemporary issues related to clergy couples. One of the tragic mistakes the Church has made in the past has been to treat marriage theoretically and legally and to make rules and regulations, often put together by celibate monks and priests, which simply did not relate to the interpersonal realities of the everyday lives of husbands and wives.

What, then, in the daily experience of the clergy couple, are the distinctive qualities of their relationship that make it Christian?

We were asked recently to contribute a chapter on "Marital Spirituality" to a Catholic symposium, and this proved to be a challenging assignment. You might like as a couple, before going further, to discuss how you would answer this question. Let us share with you what we came up with:

1. *We believe that it was God who brought us together in*

the first place. As we have already said, it seems unthinkable for Christians to see such a significant event as the choice of a life partner as a matter of blind chance. In this connection read again Genesis 24, the beautiful and moving story of how Isaac and Rebekah were brought together. In our time marriages are not by arrangement but by free choice; but the basic underlining principle, that the guiding hand of God is at work in the making of such a momentous decision, remains as valid today as it was in those early times.

Of course we could not suggest that, if we had not married each other, we could not each have married someone else and made a success of it. We don't subscribe to the one-and-only theory that Plato expounded and that the romantic fairy tales propagate. What we do believe, though, is that we were each led to marry one of perhaps a number of persons of the opposite sex with whom we might creatively have fulfilled our vocations. And this awareness has sustained us when the going was hard and motivated us to work diligently at our relationship in the confidence that all obstacles could eventually be overcome.

2. *We believe that our continuing life together is part of the divine purpose.* This follows naturally from our first affirmation. We do not look only for happiness in our life together. We see that as an ephemeral goal. Rather, we believe that if we find and fulfill together our true vocations, happiness will be the inevitable reward. In order to do this, we have both sought to qualify ourselves, separately and together, for the fields of service where we could use our natural gifts and the skills we have learned. We have always believed that the service-oriented life is the truly fulfilled life, and our actual experience has confirmed this over and over again.

3. *We believe that we have a witness to bear together.* One reason for our strong motivation to strive for continuing growth in our own relationship has been that we couldn't offer to others what we didn't possess ourselves. We see around us many couples who, with the best of intentions, are failing to make their marriages work successfully. We don't blame them, but we do feel

compassion for them. We know that today we are greatly increasing our knowledge of the very difficult task of achieving close relationships that are mutually fulfilling, and we want to make these new insights available to other married couples. But we know that we can do this with far greater persuasiveness if we are using these resources ourselves and finding them to be effective.

Our culture is unable to do what it should be doing to help marriages to succeed because the whole field of intimate relationships is shrouded in taboos, allowing misconceptions to live on which are totally discredited. Unfortunately, these taboos are firmly sustained in most churches, and the result is that Christian married couples cannot reach out for understanding and help. We are convinced that some of us must have the courage to bring the realities of our own marriages out into the open, acknowledging our humanness, owning our struggles, but also bearing our witness that we now have answers that are beginning to be effective. We shall have more to say about this in the next chapter.

4. *We believe that our shared life must have a sacrificial quality.* Many of the cults of today are based on the concept that happiness is getting everything you want. A Christian writer, reviewing a book that promoted this popular philosophy, called it "Christianity without the cross." American culture in the era of affluence has increased our dependency on luxuries that promise to take the struggle out of life—although in fact this promise is seldom fulfilled.

While it is true that some of the early Christians carried the ascetic ideal to absurd lengths, our fear is that nowadays we are in danger of going to the opposite extreme. We, ourselves, have rediscovered through the Quaker heritage how much the New Testament stresses the need for simplicity and frugality. We have also learned that if we are to serve other people successfully we can do it best by not appearing to be superior, which only makes them feel inadequate or envious, but by living unpretentiously and enabling them to feel comfortable in our presence. We must admit that, while we think pastors and their families should be assured of a reasonably comfortable standard of living, we become disturbed when they clamor for the status symbols that today represent the worship of the golden calf.

5. *We believe that our Christian marriage must find spiritual expression.* One of the concerns of the clergy couples we have worked with is their inability to talk freely together about their personal religious feelings and experiences and to sustain a meaningful plan for shared devotion. We can sympathize with them in this, because for years we tried all kinds of readings and prayers and found that they tended to become artificial and meaningless. Yet a Christian couple living together need some way of realizing the presence of God together in the everyday setting of their home, as well as in the formal worship of the church.

Some clergy couples are able to read the Bible and pray together very comfortably and find it to be a deeply meaningful experience. Many, however, have great difficulty in doing so—no less than 40 percent of the pastors and 55 percent of the wives in our study checked family devotions as an area of difficulty. For some of these the focus of the difficulty may be holding the attention of their children, but we suspect that the trouble goes deeper than that.

It has seemed to us that congregational worship in the church depends on some elements that do not make it fit easily into the more informal and intimate setting of the home. Here again, we found the answer for ourselves in the Quaker tradition, where the sharing of silence enables each worshiper, according to his or her own personal needs, to seek communion with God separately and privately, yet supported by the awareness that the others are also sharing in the experience. As we sometimes jokingly put it to our colleagues in other denominations, "You spend prayer time talking to God. We prefer to spend it in listening to him." We offer this suggestion, for what it is worth, to any whom it may help. It is very easy, and natural, to sit together at home, both engaged in worship, but using the time in whatever way best meets his or her personal need.

The devotional time together is appropriately concluded with the kiss of peace.

We are well aware that what we have said about ways to make marriage more distinctively Christian may be of little help to couples who are alienated and unhappy with each other. Tremendous barriers can build up through the years as a result of progressive disillusionment and discouragement, and to such couples the kind of picture Tertullian painted can only seem exasperating, because it is so far removed from their present reality that is seems impossible of attainment.

In our next chapter we shall offer resources that have served to break this kind of deadlock for many clergy couples. We believe that there are few marital deadlocks that are in fact impossible to break through. What is best of all about the marriages of Christians is that they have the power of divine love to call upon when human love falters and fails. The trouble is not that God withholds this power until we deserve it, but rather that pride and hardness of heart bring us to the point where we are not willing to stretch out our hands to receive it.

When the realization that we are far short of where we ought to be sweeps over us with numbing force, the only thing we can do is to start from where we are—but to *start* and so break through the paralysis. As William Douglas (Pastoral Psychology, December 1961) expresses it, "A commitment is required which is intense without being rigid, humble but not humorless, which leads to doing the best that one limited, fumbling human being can do, leaving the rest in God's hands."

Our exercise for you this time follows the same pattern as before. Each separately should make a personal response, and then guess at the other's response, before coming together for sharing and discussion.

1. In your thinking about Christian marriage, do you favor ( ) the hierarchical model? ( ) the companionship model? ( ) a mixture of both? In your opinion, does your partner also favor the model you favor? ( ) yes ( ) no.

2. When you married each other, did you feel that God

had brought you together, as part of his plan for your lives? ( ) yes ( ) no. How do you think your partner would respond? ( ) yes ( ) no.

3. Do you feel that your relationship, as it is now, could be seen as an example of what a Christian marriage is like? ( ) yes ( ) no. What do you think your partner's response would be ( ) yes ( ) no.

4. Do you feel that your shared life as a Christian couple should have a sacrificial quality? ( ) yes ( ) no. How do you think your partner would respond? ( ) yes ( ) no.

5. Have you as a Christian couple found a way in which, comfortably and helpfully, you can worship together? ( ) yes ( ) no. What would you expect your partner's response to be? ( ) yes ( ) no.

CHAPTER XI

New Resources for Couple Growth

In this chapter we get down to what is sometimes called the "nitty-gritty," which our dictionary defines as "the hard core of the matter." We will divest the pastor of his clerical robes, of his degrees and diplomas. We will take him out of sight and earshot of his congregation. We will likewise temporarily take the pastor's wife away from any offices she holds in the church, from any occupation or vocation she pursues in the community. We will have them pack up only the basic baggage they may need for a very informal occasion and drive to a designated destination. There they will be spending several days with five or six other couples (not necessarily clergy couples) whom they have probably never met before and may never meet again.

In that setting, they can focus their attention entirely on the one thing that really matters—the quality of their relationship. Now there is no need to pose, to hide behind pretenses or defenses. Now they can face together, in a secluded and supportive atmosphere, the ultimate questions, Is our relationship all that we want it to be? Are *we* a truly loving couple? And if not, what can we do to make it so?

As the group assembles for the first session of a marriage enrichment retreat, the following objectives of their time together will be exhibited:

(1)   To take a sincere, honest look at our marriage, *as it is now*.

(2)   To identify the areas in which we want our marriage to *grow in the next year*.

(3)   To gain the necessary *insights*, and to acquire the necessary *skills*, to make our future growth possible.

Another poster on the wall will give the ground rules that will determine the way the group functions:

(1) We share our experiences—*not* our opinions.

(2) No confrontation—all participation is voluntary.

(3) No diagnosing, analyzing, or advice giving—unless requested by the couple.

We, as the leader couple, will make it clear that we are participating facilitators—not leaders in any authoritative sense. We, just like the other couples in the group, bring only our marriage, and we are ready to be open in sharing our humanness, our struggles, our hopes and expectations. We will give no orders. We will simply, as facilitators, offer suggestions, which may or may not be accepted by the group. We are committed only to the objectives and the ground rules.

In the hours that follow, the couples in the group will try to identify their particular needs, and out of these we will make an agenda. There will be plenty of opportunity for each couple to be alone together, in private dialogue, to work through some of their personal issues. There will also be opportunity for couples who wish to do so to dialogue together in the group, by way of sharing their "growing edges"; and other couples may identify with them by dialoguing where *they* are in dealing with the same issues. We as leaders will demonstrate the dialogue by taking some issue on the agenda and sharing how we are trying to handle it in our marriage. If no other couples wish to dialogue, there will be no need to do so. It is a very useful method, but not essential.

At appropriate times we will suggest exercises to do that may help—either group exercises to do together or couple exercises to do privately like the ones we gave you in the last two chapters. We may explain some aspect of couple interaction about which the group needs guidance. But always the group will make the decision. If as leaders we do not know what to do next or feel that we are not making progress, we'll say so and ask the group to help us. The group always responds.

Marriage enrichment retreats and growth groups are of many kinds. We have briefly described the model we personally favor. Our preference is for as little structure as possible, but we will use structure if that seems to be needed. The essence of the process is the same in all valid marriage enrichment programs—to promote the three objectives we have listed.

As the retreat proceeds, the couples become united in a sense of common purpose. As trust develops over time, they find they can be more and more open with each other, and as they do so they relax and a pervasive feeling of warmth develops. We all gain an awareness of having much in common as we realize that most of us have been working on the same issues, and it is very rewarding to be able to share our experiences—to learn from, and be encouraged by each other.

That is as far as we can take you, in a book, toward experiencing a marriage enrichment retreat. We can, however, give you some idea of what this kind of experience has meant to clergy couples who have actually participated in it. Here are some anonymous evaluations from such couples:

The experience has been very fulfilling and meaningful for our marriage relationship. It will be a joy now to go back to our church and share some of the insights that we have gained. Our marriage will never be the same again, for you have provided the needed stimulus for its ongoing enrichment.

This has been a very valuable experience. It should have the greatest potential in developing positive, constructive development of the marriages of those of us who have shared in it; and, as a carry-over, a vital impact on the families within the churches in which we minister.

Specially helpful has been the sharing time with other clergy couples. My wife and I have set the stage for our further growth, as well as for sharing with others what this experience has meant to us.

This has been a unique experience for me. Even though I thought, and still think, that we have a healthy marriage, I have gained much new insight about myself and my partner. We have charted some areas in which we will work together to make our relationship even better than it was.

This has been a true godsend. After twenty-two years, our

marriage was at an impasse. We knew what we needed to do, but just didn't have the proper tools, nor the motivation. Now we have both and are full of hope.

This has indeed been an enriching experience. I needed the challenge, and the time to act on it—for myself as well as our marriage. I appreciated our being treated as mature adults wanting to grow. I only wish that many other clergy couples could have this beautiful experience.

I have enjoyed, in a very special way, these hours with my wife, and we have committed ourselves to practicing at home what we have learned here. We have experienced excitement and joy at the privilege of being part of this experience.

This experience has been for me a breath of fresh air and cup of cold water amidst a desert wasteland. For my wife and myself, it came at a much needed time. It has brought us light and hope, and we now go forward in anticipation and expectation as we launch anew into the building of intimacy.

It has been very timely for our marriage to participate in this experience. Our sense of renewal has been tremendous. We have been challenged and inspired.

I came ready to learn and to grow, and I have not been disappointed. My partner and I have some new handles for our future growth. It has been an affirming time.

We attended this retreat because we wanted to improve a very good marriage. You have given us so many resources that I am sure we will do just that. We have made a new commitment to each other and to our family.

This has been a rare privilege. The experience was refreshing, helpful, and on the cutting edge. It has been most affirming of our own marriage, and has inspired us with new energy to serve the marriages and families in our parish.

I can hardly believe that so much could have happened in so short a time. I can think of nothing more valuable than that pastors and their wives everywhere could have an experience of this kind. We shall go home with a new commitment to our growth together.

Obviously there is a dynamic at work here that is powerful and pervasive. Relaxing the social taboos and enabling couples to be open and honest with each other, releases resources that never become available in our normal social interactions. Anyone who has experienced this realizes the exciting possibilities that are opened up when we create a setting in which couples can encourage and help each other to work together for better marriages.

But that is not the only factor that is at work. In recent years, too, there has been an explosion of new knowledge about close relationships, coming from the behavioral sciences. The retreat certainly provides a helpful setting where couples can look at their marriages as they now are, and as they want them to be. But the third objective of the retreat—the gaining of new insights and skills—is made possible only by much clearer understanding of the dynamics of marital interaction. So, if we can't take you to a retreat (though we might motivate you to go yourselves!) we *can* summarize for you some of the new and vital knowledge that is now available.

We shall see that "vital" is the right word if we look back to the needs that were expressed by the clergy couples in our study. The major ones were in the areas of more effective couple communication, the management of positive and negative emotions, and the resolving of conflict. This was no surprise to us. On the agendas of scores of retreats we have led over the years, these are the issues that have come up again and again and again.

We have more than a suspicion that the concern of clergy couples about unreasonable expectations of the congregation is closely connected with behavior, which reveals that they are unable to handle their negative emotions constructively. We quoted one husband who wanted to "blow his top" once in a while, and a wife who didn't want anyone to hear her yelling at her children. What's wrong with both of these behaviors is not so much that they are wicked or unchristian, but that they are unproductive and damaging to good family relationships. There are much better ways of handling these tensions, and they can be learned.

We therefore believe that we can now meet most of the critical needs of clergy couples. That may seem a big claim to make; yet we *do* make it with a good deal of confidence. We shall devote most of the remainder of the chapter to sketching, as clearly as we can in brief space, what we now know about the critical areas.

Our view is that there are three essentials for a successful marriage. With them, the chances for a couple are very good. Without them, unless expectations are quite low, the chances are very poor.

The first essential is *a commitment to growth* on the part of both husband and wife. The process of fitting two human personalities together, in a close interaction that enables them to become what they are capable of becoming, both as persons and as a couple, is very complex. The sad truth is that most couples struggle at it for awhile, find their efforts defeated, give up and settle for a partial adjustment as the best they can hope for. In most cases they are not to blame for their failure. It was simply that they couldn't do the job, because they didn't have the tools.

Growth in a relationship means the willingness to *change*—to make modifications in your attitudes and behavior in order to bring about the smooth "fit" that is necessary for harmony.

But *can* people change? Yes, and no. You cannot change your basic personality pattern—that was built in quite early in life. What you *can* do, however, is to change the way you *act*, in order to further your best interests and goals. One of the most startling discoveries that has emerged from recent studies of older people is that they are able to change their behavior up to the day of their death! Sayings like "An old dog can't learn new tricks," are not really true.

Changed behavior, however, occurs only under two conditions. There must be the necessary *motivation* to start, and the motivation must be sustained by providing adequate *rewards*. So the couple must begin by making a solemn commitment to each other to do the necessary work together in order to make relational change possible. The first task of marriage enrichment is for a couple to make that commitment to each other.

The second essential for a successful marriage is *an effective communication system*. The truth is that married couples generally communicate very poorly; and according to a study reported in 1973 by the Family Service Association of America, this is a major factor in marriage failure.

However, couples can now be trained, comparatively easily, to communicate effectively; although it usually takes them some time to develop the new skills until they become habitual. Across the country, increasing numbers of couples are taking one or another of the communication courses that are being made available to them. We would strongly recommend you to consider doing so. The most popular program, *Couple Communication*, involves six or seven couples in twelve hours of training by a qualified instructor. For information write to Interpersonal Communication Programs, Inc., 300 Clifton Avenue, Minneapolis, Mn. 55403.

What would you learn in such a course? First, you would be shown how to develop self-awareness—to listen to the constant stream of *feelings* that surge within you, providing you with vital information about what is going on in your inner life. Many people just don't listen to their feelings, they reject them, deny them, project them, displace them. If you don't tune in to your feelings, you are not in charge of your own life. It is as simple as that.

Next, you would learn to share your feelings, as well as your thoughts and intentions, with your marriage partner. Two people cannot relate fully to each other at surface level. They have to know what is going on *inside* each other. You can easily guess wrong and say or do something that hurts or alienates your partner. Most couples who take marriage enrichment seriously schedule a sharing time each day when they can open up their inner selves to each other. This can very appropriately, for a clergy couple, be part of their shared time for worship. Getting in touch with God and with each other go beautifully together.

A vital part of good communication is to be able to share negative feelings without attacking each other and getting into a fight. We now know that there are four different communication styles, and that when couples can learn to use the right ones in the right combination, negative feelings can be handled constructively. This represents a major breakthrough in our understanding of how people interact in close relationships.

There are other resources. By learning to complete their communication cycles, a couple can develop a tool which, if properly used, will prevent them from ever again being involved in a serious misunderstanding. And by learning to affirm each other frequently, they can change the whole atmosphere of their relationship from negative to positive.

These skills are not beyond the reach of ordinary couples, and with determination and full cooperation they can be learned and practiced until they become almost habitual.

When we recall that 50 percent of the husbands in our study and 62 percent of the wives checked "couple communication" as an area in which they needed help, it can readily be seen that we have some good news for them.

The third essential for a successful marriage is learning *how to use conflict creatively*. Our culture has taught us to regard conflict in a loving relationship as something highly undesirable, to be avoided wherever possible. We now know that this is a tragic error. In recent years, psychologists have recognized that an interpersonal conflict is really a growth point—a clash of wills that identifies a difference in the partners that needs to be examined and adjusted. It is like a squeak in your car engine that warns you that something needs to be fixed, or the functioning of the motor will deteriorate.

By handling conflict creatively, therefore, a couple can promote growth in their relationship and make it more secure. The process is not simple. It involves, among other things, understanding anger in marriage as raw material, which can be used to increase love and intimacy between husband and wife.

With this new knowledge, we can offer something really effective to meet critical needs in a high proportion of clergy couples. Sixty-nine percent of wives and 50 percent of husbands listed the handling of negative emotions as an area in which they needed help.

We cannot elaborate this further here. It would take

another book to explain in detail how to use these new resources that are now available. Anyway, we have already written that book. It is *How to Have a Happy Marriage*, a workbook in which we invite the couple to devote twenty-four hours of their time, spaced over a six-week period, to enrich their marriage. They can do this together at home. But it is much better for a group of couples to do it together, meeting once a week to share experiences and report progress to one another.

We should add that the skills and tools we are talking about here are practical resources that we ourselves, and hundreds of other couples known to us, have used effectively, and are still using, to promote the growth of our own marriages.

It is our conviction that most of the difficulties that married couples get into in other areas—sex, money management, decision making—are the direct or indirect result of poor communication systems and the inability to cope creatively with conflict. So any plan for the general improvement of your relationship should begin, we suggest, with the three essentials.

If what we have said gives you the impression that the achievement of a loving, creative marriage is a difficult task, you can say that again. The romantic legend that a wedding ceremony automatically brings deep and lasting happiness to a couple is not only a misleading message; it is a cruel lie. Happiness in marriage is like every other achievement in life; it has to be worked for and earned. And even that alone is not enough. You must also have an understanding of the process.

We therefore encourage you to find out all you can about marriage enrichment and to get involved. Even if you think your marriage is already so good that it couldn't possibly be better, you would find it very valuable to go through an enrichment experience, because you would then have new resources to offer to other couples who may need your help.

However, supposing your marriage is in really poor shape, and all we have been talking about only gives you a sense of frustration and despair. You know deep down that you need much more than a weekend with other couples who are seeking only to make their good marriages better.

In that event, marriage counseling is the answer for you. And we hope that increasingly the churches will make it possible for clergy couples who need marital therapy to get it, in circumstances in which their need will be compassionately understood and their right to privacy respected. We hope also that some financial aid may be available if this is needed. It is in the best interest of the churches that pastors and their wives should be in good marital, as well as physical, health; and nothing takes a heavier toll of a pastor's emotional resources than being unhappy at home and not being able to do anything about it. If you two, as a clergy couple, have accepted your vocations to the family and the church, and are unable to fulfill those vocations because you are in a sea of trouble, the whole fellowship of Christian believers should be caringly and lovingly behind you and beside you. What you are suffering, any of us might have suffered; and you need and deserve our compassion and our active help. If we adopt a holier-than-thou attitude, we are acting more like Pharisees than Christian believers.

Now we invite you to do what we call the "I want" exercise. Put down three headings, with space between, on a sheet of paper—"I Want for Me," "I Want for You," and "I Want for Us." Now take ten or fifteen minutes to list under each heading what you would like to see accomplished in the next year—for you personally, for your partner personally, for you together as a couple.

When you have both made your list, come together and share them. See how accurately you have judged each other's needs, and your joint needs. In a marriage enrichment retreat, we follow up this exercise by inviting the couple to take some time to make a growth plan for the next twelve months. One way is to merge your lists, agreeing on what seems reasonably attainable, and putting it all in a written statement. Then, if you feel you can both sign it, do so. This signifies a serious commitment made by both of you that you will help and support each other in pursuing your agreed goals.

Keep this growth plan and check up from time to time to see what progress you are making. Change the plan at any time if you need to.

You have now taken the first vital step toward an enriched marriage. You have made a commitment to growth.

Let us conclude this part of the book by saying that you, far more than any other person or persons ever could, must take responsibility for the quality of your marriage. Resources are available to you today which we have never had before in human history. If you need them, but don't use them, you must accept responsibility for that decision; just as a person who ignores the rules for good health must assume responsibility for what happens. By ignoring these resources, you might not be only inflicting needless suffering on yourselves, but also denying others the more effective ministry that can be offered by a warm, loving, and united couple.

What we are trying to say in this book is that clergy marriages ought to be really good marriages, reflecting in human terms the creative love of God that is our message to mankind. This is the *vocation* that you as a couple have chosen. It is your good fortune to have rich resources at your disposal that can take you a long way toward achieving this exciting and rewarding goal.

CHAPTER XII

The Clergy Family

King Edward VI of England came to the throne in the year 1547, at the age of nine, succeeding his famous father King Henry VIII. He was poorly equipped to rule. His health soon deteriorated, and he died of consumption in the year 1553, at fifteen years of age.

Yet his short reign was important because it brought, for the first time, full and free permission to the English clergy to marry. Although Martin Luther had acted in Germany to end the Catholic ban on clergy marriage, Henry VIII had opposed this for the English clergy. However, when Edward VI came to the throne, marriage became legally permissible, and many clergy took advantage of this.

Unfortunately, the young king was succeeded by his half sister Mary, who earned the title of "Bloody Mary." In her fanatical zeal for the Catholic faith she reversed the law and insisted that all married clergy should put away their wives and undergo public humiliation for their immoral behavior. Rather than do this, one in four of all clergy left the Church. Others, refusing to renounce their Protestant faith, were accused of heresy, and put to death—usually by being publicly burned at the stake.

One of these was Rowland Taylor, vicar of Hadley in Suffolk. The record shows that he had been married before he entered the ministry and that he and his wife had had nine children. He was thrown into prison, tried, and condemned to death. The sentence was to be carried out publicly in the parish that he had served as pastor.

On a cold, dark morning, Rowland Taylor was taken from the prison where he had been kept. Out in the street his wife and children were waiting. He embraced them tenderly, and then all knelt down together in the street and repeated the Lord's Prayer; after which, "with calmness and courage," he was led away to be burned to death in the presence of his former congregation.

It may seem incredible to us today that such things could happen. But Taylor was one of many martyrs who, in those dark days, laid down their lives for what they believed. We tell this story to remind all clergy couples that their right to enjoy the blessings of a Christian family was won by courage and sacrifice.

In this chapter we want to affirm the clergy family. In gathering the material for this book we have been made aware of many difficulties and disadvantages that clergy couples have to meet. Yet at the same time we have been deeply moved by awareness of all that being a clergy family can mean—the rich heritage of the past; the shining examples to which any clergy couple can look for inspiration; the exciting possibilities that lie in a shared life of service to others. All this is opened up for a couple who accept God's call and go forth hand in hand together to experience for themselves, and to proclaim to others, the gospel message that has been for long centuries, and still is today, the greatest hope for that better world for which all people of goodwill wait and work.

It may be appropriate at this point to quote a few of the many advantages of being a clergy couple which were listed by the couples in our study:

"Being called of God to serve him in a special capacity."
"Having a singleness of purpose in our lives."
"Surrounded by the love of Christian friends."
"Living within the circle of God's will."
"Encouragement and support for continuing emotional and spiritual growth."
"Opportunity to work as a team on tasks of eternal significance."
"A strong sense of purpose and mission in life."
"A wonderful opportunity to live the life of grace in the power of the Lord."
"A constant challenge to live up to high ideals."
"Being part of a loving fellowship of believers."

"Satisfaction of helping people in the very best way they
  can be helped—finding God's love."
"A people-oriented vocation that really has the answers."

These are quoted almost at random. Similar responses
occur over and over again.

Other investigators found the same warm approval among
clergy couples. William Douglas sums up his study of
ministers' wives saying; "With all these qualifications, what
may be observed about the values and goals of the American
Protestant MW's who participated in this study? Most
obvious was their religious commitment and desire to be of
assistance in their husbands' ministry. They wanted to serve
God and husband, and believed in the purposes of the
Church, whether or not they had experienced a specific
sense of call to be a MW and/or to a Church-related
vocation."

Ann and Hale Schroer, in *The Christian Ministry* (July
1971) listed four "strengths" of the clergy marriage:

1. The events of the day are shared with a common point
of reference.

2. The wife is not left out of her husband's world, as in
the case of most other professionals.

3. Both are often involved together in the same tasks,
with the same goals.

4. Less "fragmentation" of life—all the pieces can be
"put together."

Denton, summing up his impressions of the clergy wives
with whom he worked, says simply, "There was purpose in
their lives."

The foundation stone of the clergy family is the unity of
husband and wife. They are, as Tertullian expressed it,
"One in hope, one in desire, one in the way of life they
follow, one in the religion they practice."

As a united couple, you will have a secure base. You will
not have to expend energy and time in anxious efforts to
manipulate each other, in struggling to clear up misunder-
standings, in nursing grievances, in keeping up petty
deceptions, in struggling with painful and exhausting

conflict. It is highly gratifying to reach a point at which, although there will still be differences and disagreements that generate anger and pain, you know how to deal with these situations and clear them up quickly and effectively as they arise.

From this secure base you can turn outward to face the world, knowing that you stand together and support each other. Now you are really able to fulfill your vocations, to give the service to others to which you have committed yourselves.

But first, on the secure base of your unity as a couple, your task is to build a Christian family. If you have children, they are part of your very selves, and your first joint ministry is to them. Somehow you must manage to include them in your unity—with one arm around each other, each to extend the other arm to draw your children within the embrace that will include you all.

Today, this is no easy task. In our open society, many of the methods of the past simply will not work anymore.

Listen again to Charles Bridges as he speaks to pastors about their family responsibilities—in the year 1829:

If a man knows not how to rule his own house, how shall he take care of the Church of God? For he cannot reasonably expect to perform in his parish the work which he has not cared to accomplish at home. . . . Though he cannot convey grace to his children, at least he can enforce restraint. . . . He can inculcate upon them the responsibility of promoting his Ministry . . . showing, that the principles of their father's house and Ministry are the rule of their conduct. . . . With respect to children—we must be careful to exhibit a clear practical illustration of the rules of order, submission, and indulgence, which we give to our people. . . . The correctness of our family system becomes to a great extent the standard of our parish; while its inconsistencies too often furnish excuse for the neglect of duty, or the positive indulgence in sin. . . . If the parsonage does not show the pattern as well as the doctrine, exhortations from thence will only excite the ridicule of the ungodly. . . . It is therefore of great moment to repress all expensiveness of habits, studied attention to orna- ment, and every mark of pleasure or vanity. (pp. 154-56)

That was over a hundred and fifty years ago. Notice what is being said and the language used. The minister must "rule" his family, so that they will provide a "practical illustration" of what he preaches in the pulpit. If he cannot persuade his children to do this, he must "enforce restraint." The goal is to have them demonstrate "correctness," "consistent conduct," and "submission" and to avoid all appearance of "neglect of duty," "indulgence in sin," "pleasure," or "vanity."

Consider how profoundly our world has changed, and how our interpretation of Christian behavior has changed, in a century and a half. The parsonage child of 1829 lived in a very restricted environment. His life was closely supervised. There were no movies, no radio, no television to confront him with standards and values other than those of home and church. His reading was censored so that he picked up no worldly notions. He seldom went far from home. There were no railroads, no automobiles, not even a bicycle. His friends were probably carefully screened. Any evidence of getting out of line in his speech or behavior brought penalties that made it necessary to conform outwardly, however he might rebel inwardly.

How different is the child of today! From an early age he is exposed, even within the seclusion of his own home, to the secular values of a secular society. We all know that many preschool children spend a great deal of time watching TV. In public school he will meet other children from homes where very different standards prevail. As he grows older, he may well find his associations with the youth culture as powerful in their impact as those of his home. The hard line between religion and worldliness has been largely erased for him, so he must somehow work out for himself the life-style that seems to serve him best. Far from pleasure being evil, he is constantly encouraged to have fun. He is aware of something called sin, but its nature is vague and confused; because sex, violence, and self-centered behavior are everywhere paraded as being acceptable, if not even commendable, by people who enjoy public approval and popularity. Traditional Christian virtues like modesty, humility, and self-denial are ridiculed. The message is rather that dress should be flamboyant, behavior arrogant, and every want loudly asserted. Even dishonesty is half admired. Many consider it smart to steal or defraud if they can get away with it.

What then is Christian parenthood, and how does it function in today's world?

We certainly cannot for long rule our children today. When modern parents try to "enforce restraint," the children may rebel, rally the support of their peers, even run away from home. Today's youngsters are not impressed by ideas of "submission" and "correctness." They live in a world where it is "neat" to "assert yourself," to "do your own thing."

In other words, we must substitute something else for dominance and power. Is that, then, a great misfortune? We don't think so. It is very interesting that Bridges should say that the Christian parent "cannot convey grace to his children," and therefore he must "enforce restraint." Why can he not convey grace? Surely the conveying of grace, through parental love and devotion, is just what Christian parenthood should be all about.

Can we put together some ground rules for Christian parenthood? There was little on this subject in the literature on clergy families that we read. But we can at least try to establish some basic principles. In our opinion, there are four of them.

1. *The key to effective parenthood is a loving marriage.* It is strange how frequently this fundamental principle is overlooked. When parents love each other with deep, satisfying, and tender devotion, they inevitably create a warm, secure climate in the home that is the ideal setting for the healthy emotional growth of a child. In our opinion, no amount of scientific knowledge, no degree of efficient organization, no surfeit of material resources, can compensate for the lack of that overflow to their children of love and joy, which is continually generated by a couple whose relationship to each other is rich and creative.

2. *Parental love should be, as far as possible, based on what Carl Rogers called "unconditional positive regard."* A child needs to be loved for his own sake, not in terms of what he contributes to his parents' needs, or what he does

to make them proud of him. For Christians this has a sound theological base: "God has shown us how much he loves us—it was while we were still sinners that Christ died for us!" (Rom. 5:8 TEV). The final certainty of a parent's love for a child comes when that parent says, in effect, "Whatever you do I will still love you. Even if you hurt me, I will still believe in your worth and will still try to help you become all that I believe you are capable of becoming." This surely is the message of the parable of the prodigal son and the very heart of the teaching of Jesus.

3. *Discipline is essentially cooperation with the child in helping him to grow.* Often a child is punished because he has been a nuisance to his parents, and they are acting vengefully. The child is always aware when this is so, and inwardly he reacts accordingly. True discipline should always be for the child's own good, and this should always be openly recognized and understood. When our children were young, we made a family rule that no punishment would be inflicted until it had been acknowledged by the child as fair, and we were amazed to discover how keen a sense of justice the child often displayed. This also has a theological base—the Lord "punishes everyone he accepts as a son. When we are punished, it seems to us at the time something to make us sad. . . . Later, however, those who have been disciplined by such punishment reap the peaceful reward of a righteous life" (Heb. 12:6b, 11 TEV). So we give our children freedom, cautiously and in small amounts, encouraging them to use it constructively, as a learning experience. If they are unable to handle it, or we think they are, we restrain them till they are more mature. If they handle it wisely, we reward them by giving them more freedom next time. But it is always a cooperative process between parent and child.

4. *In relating to their children, Christian parents are open and honest about themselves.* This is the best of all examples we can set for our children. The old authoritative type of parenthood was based on putting on a "front," and the children saw through it immediately. It probably represents progress that the modern parent can no longer operate from a posture of power and dominance. We earn

our children's respect far more effectively by being sincere about our own shortcomings and struggles, while at the same time demonstrating that we are continually seeking to improve, and even asking our children to help us in the process. We ourselves found it helpful, when occasionally we punished our children in anger, to apologize to them later and ask for their forgiveness. We were simply acknowledging that we were human, as they were, and they never lost their respect for us on that account.

If we seek to practice these basic ground rules for Christian parenthood, can we be assured that our children will choose our values, rather than those of the secular world that surrounds us? We cannot be certain. But if we have faith that our values are real and have the courage to live by them, we shall have a much better chance of communicating them than by the exercise of power. What our children learn from us is not so much what we tell them in our words, but what we tell them in our deeds. We cannot protect them from the impact of other values in these days, not even in early childhood. We can only hope and pray that the strength of our love will sustain them. In adolescence, as they move toward independence, they must try their wings, learn to make their own decisions, take over and manage their own lives. They may make mistakes and get hurt. But if they know that our love is unconditional, we shall have done all we can do, and all we have a right to do, to influence the direction of their lives.

Those who write about PKs (pastors' kids) invariably acknowledge that, with a few regrettable exceptions, they turn out well. As early as 1908, James Oswald Dykes wrote in his book *The Christian Minister and His Duties*: "It is notorious that a high percentage of those who achieve marked success in professional or business careers come from the homes of the clergy. The manse has proved itself a fruitful nursery for the pulpit. Not seldom does ministerial office tend to become hereditary." (p.75)

Harmon informs us that in *Who's Who* there are more sons of ministers listed than of any other profession. Jack Hamm, a Christian cartoonist, affirms that the same is true of the Hall of Fame. If this is so, we need not be surprised.

Kathleen Nyberg drily sums up the situation thus, "There is so much evidence that the children of parsonage homes enjoy a fuller life than the average, we ought to stop sympathizing and begin congratulating them on their good fortune" (P. 31).

The time pressures on the pastor, and the hours when he is most busy, should not be allowed to deprive his children of the close contacts that both he and they desire. Unfortunately, the extensive literature about the ministry says very little about this. We found only two specific references. One was by Charles William Stewart, who says, "Because of the pressures of work, the minister expects the partner to be both mother and father to the children. I have heard ministers' spouses actually say that their young children ask who the stranger is who spends time at their home on Saturday morning."

The other reference is from Daniel Walker who makes an eloquent plea for the children of pastors, "There are men who are so dominated by a drive to fulfill their ministerial obligations that their families consistently come out at the short end. Probably these preachers do not realize how desperately their children want some attention from their father, and how deep the hurt is when they are consistently pushed aside. One preacher's small son offered his father ten cents an hour to stay home and play with him!"

An equal hazard for mothers could develop as more and more clergy wives become involved in full-time work outside the home. The Mattis study, however, was reassuring on this point. Of all the wives with full-time jobs, only 4 percent had a child under five.

The lighter side of the pastor as parent appears in several stories. One told by J. C. Wynn refers to two daughters of the manse, one of whom said to the other, "You'd better be careful what you do, or Daddy will tell about it in a sermon." Another (unidentified) tells how a pastor's wife said to their daughter, "Have you read that book I lent you?" She replied, "Well, I did start it, but when the hero decided to be a minister, I quit, because I knew nothing interesting would happen to him after that."

No discussion of the clergy family should leave out Martin Luther, whose marriage to Katherine von Bora in 1532 defied the Church's rule of clerical celibacy. Roland H. Bainton in *Here I Stand, A Life of Martin Luther,* chapter 17, gives us some delightful glimpses of the great reformer as husband and father.

In May 1526, a letter from Luther to a distinguished friend announced, "There is about to be born a child of a monk and a nun. Such a child must have a great lord for godfather. Therefore I am inviting you. I cannot be precise as to the time."

On June 8 he declared, "My dear Katie brought into the world yesterday by God's grace at two o'clock a little son." Soon after, he wrote again, "Hans is cutting his teeth and beginning to make a joyous nuisance of himself. These are the joys of marriage of which the pope is not worthy."

The Luthers had six children in all—three boys and three girls. Six of their own, that is. In addition, they raised four homeless orphans. To help meet the family budget, they took in students as paying guests. There were times when the household grew to as many as twenty-five persons.

Were there tensions in this pioneering clergy family? Indeed there were. After all his theorizing, practical experience brought Luther down to earth. He admitted that family life was demanding and began to talk of marriage as "a school for character." There were constant struggles to balance the budget. For Katie, the strain of bearing children, added to her other burdens, was hard to take. Martin had to help as best he could. Once, when hanging out diapers, he caused great amusement to the neighbors. "Let them laugh," he exclaimed, "God and the angels smile in heaven!"

Marital conflict? Of course. "Good God," he once exclaimed, "What a lot of trouble there is in marriage! Adam has made a mess of our nature. Think of all the squabbles Adam and Eve must have had in the course of their nine hundred years." Modern clergy couples will recognize Martin's complaint about coming home after preaching four times, lecturing to students, dealing with all kinds of responsibilities and wanting only to relax and go to sleep; but Katie, after a day of caring for the children, looking after animals, and giving orders to servants, was ready for some adult conversation and asked "Doctor, is the prime minister of Prussia the Duke's brother?"

Luther loved his children, but they could also cause him vexation. He is reported as saying to one of them, "What have you done that I should love you so? You have disturbed the whole household with your bawling." And once, referring to his family, he cried, "Christ said we must become as little children to enter the kingdom of heaven. Dear God, this is too much. Have we got to become such idiots?"

But his outbursts of exasperation were all on the surface. Many incidents show him as a loving, tender father. The most moving of all happened when Magdalene, fourteen years old, was dying. Luther prayed, "Oh God, I love her so, but thy will be done." And he said to her, "My little girl, you would like to stay with your father here and you would be glad to go to your Father in heaven?" Her reply was, "Yes, dear father, as God wills." Katie stood by, transfixed with silent grief, while Martin took Magdalena in his arms and held her close until she sank into her last sleep.

Literature on the Christian ministry since Luther's time has given far too little attention to the clergy family. But here and there a writer has paused to consider the vital influence of the pastor's family upon the effectiveness of his ministry. We may well conclude by quoting two of these—first, James Oswald Dykes, who enjoyed a ministry of no less than fifty years duration. Here is what he wrote in the year 1908:

The reflex influence of a family home upon the minister's own spirit, in the way either of sustaining him in his daily duties or of incapacitating him for their discharge, is almost incalculable. . . . In no other calling is a man so dependent on home influences for keeping him day by day in the fittest condition for doing his public duty in the holy ministry; simply because in no other calling does the quality of work depend so absolutely on the moral and religious state of the workman. It needs no words to show that the quiet punctual orderliness of a well-conducted household must contribute materially to maintain serenity of temper, with a constant readiness for duties which can only be performed when one's spirit is at leisure from itself. . . . To be able to go forth from home to one's work in a self-collected and reverent mood, and to return to it as an arbor of refreshment where one is sure of sympathy—all this means a great deal to the busy pastor, and it is precisely this which a suitable partner and a carefully ordered household ought to furnish. (pp. 70-71)

It will be noticed that Dykes places great emphasis on the quality of the family home that is provided for the minister, with the obvious implication that this is how his wife demonstrates her love for him. That was the way it was seen in 1908, and it is all still quite true.

However, what the minister's family does for him must be balanced by what he does for them, and what they all do together. So we will balance the words of Dykes with those from a very modern book about the minister and his family. *Coping with Stress in the Minister's Home* was published by Broadman Press just as we completed the writing of this one, in 1979, and in this case, written jointly by a pastor and his wife, Robert and Mary Frances Bailey.

All families need regular, in-depth, meaningful interaction between husband and wife and parents and children. . . . Every stress described in the life of the minister culminates in the stress of the family. . . . These multiple stresses tend to create and compound stress in the lives both of the individual family members and the entire family unit.

A minister must stop and take inventory to determine his priorities. Unless he feels that his love for God is followed by his love for his family, he may be dragging his family down the drain emotionally if not spiritually . . . . Sharing vital concerns, engaging in family worship, caring for people in need, praying for one another, forgiving mistakes, demonstrating patience, allowing space to be individuals, discussing the Bible studies, and having time for each other are but a few of the ways in which the minister, his wife, and their children can implement in their life-style the concepts they publicly espouse.

Sing a song of gladness because God has called you to be special people for him. Go then and be those people. (pp.115-16, 122)

APPENDIX I

Recommendations to Denominational Officials

It was our decision, and the wish of our publishers, that this book should be addressed directly to typical clergy couples, and should try to offer them insights and resources to help them make their marriages as happy and healthy as possible. This we have tried to do in the pages you have read so far.

However, in our search for material, we were made aware of many other aspects of clergy marriages with which we could not, in the limited space available, deal directly. Since important issues of planning and policy are involved for the churches, we decided to include some of this extra material, in summary form only, in this appendix. Of necessity, what we shall have to say will be brief and sketchy. But even that seems better than making no reference at all to aspects of the subject that should be of real concern to ecclesiastical leaders, even if not to clergy couples as a whole.

We have tried to arrange this material in some sort of order, though of necessity there will be a good deal of overlapping. Our main purpose has been to draw attention to aspects of the clergy marriage that called for further investigation by church leaders and denominational officials, as they seek to formulate sound policies.

We shall deal only with the clergyman and his nonclergy wife, for reasons that will be explained later.

I. What the Denominations Are Now Doing

As part of our investigation, we sent out a questionnaire to sixty selected persons. In the main they represented Protestant denominations in the U.S.A. and Canada; but also included were a few special agencies and institutions concerned with clergy marriages.

We received twenty-two replies from denominations and eight from specialized agencies—a total of thirty, and therefore a 50 percent return.

The main purpose of the questionnaire was to find out what kinds of action had been taken to address the issue of clergy marriage. The following items represent the returns from the denominations:

What's Happening to Clergy Marriages?

Made an investigation or study	7	32%
Provided special counseling services	11	50%
Provided specific marriage enrichment programs	14	64%
Held a consultation or conference	8	36%
Published a report of some kind	7	32%
Appointed a person to explore the field	5	23%

It is probable that the denominations that responded were those most likely to have taken action, although two of them acknowledged that they had done nothing as yet. It will be seen that major moves so far have been in the field of providing marriage counseling and marriage enrichment for clergy couples—one-half and two-thirds respectively; but that about one-third of them have taken some investigative action, and one-quarter have designated a particular person to explore the field.

A number of denominations and agencies sent us copies of publications and other materials. The evidence suggests that at least some of the churches are aware of, and concerned about, the need to take more seriously their responsibility for the state of clergy marriages. As time passes, we would anticipate that further action will be taken, and that this process will accelerate.

We consider that the actions so far taken show good judgment. We would suggest that three objectives should have high priority in denominational planning:

(1) Investigate the situation thoroughly and get all the facts out in the open.

(2) Provide quality enrichment programs for as many clergy couples as possible, as a preventive measure.

(3) Provide competent counseling services, as early as possible, for clergy couples in serious trouble.

II. The Recruitment and Training of Clergy

There is urgent need to abandon, once and for all, the concept that a pastor is accepted and employed by the Church, which then takes responsibility for him; but that his wife, if he has one, is an attached appendage for whom the Church has no special responsibility or concern.

In recruiting future pastors, more attention needs to be paid, not only to the candidates' personal fitness for the exacting tasks of the ministry, but also to the personal fitness of the spouses (if any) for the exacting task of being married to a minister.

We encountered some materials (specially Booth and Bowers) which suggest that certain personality types tend more than others to seek entrance into the ministry. We also found in Morentz some provocative suggestions about the personality characteristics of clergy wives. This opens up a large and complex subject, which we deemed to be beyond the scope of this book; but it seems to call for thorough investigation if the Church is to screen out persons who are poorly equipped for the demanding callings of ministry, of clergy marriage, or of both.

The Mattis study found that 65 percent of pastors today are married either before they enter seminary or while they are in theological training, while another 10 percent marry before accepting their first pastorates. This suggests that the Church could, with tact and sensitivity, do a great deal to check that these marriages are sound before the couples have to cope with adjustment to a congregation.

The opportunity, and the responsibility, of the theological seminary are of special significance. The scholarly and thorough study made by van Arnold has never been published, but it merits the most serious consideration and could easily be replicated under present conditions.

The basic finding of van Arnold is that, in the seminary years, both members of the clergy couple are normally making three difficult adjustments at one and the same time—from late adolescence to adulthood; from singlehood to marriage; and from the secular society to the ministerial milieu. Also this combination of transitions is highly complex and often not successfully accomplished, with unfortunate consequences later. Finally, the seminary which fails to understand these adjustments and does not provide all possible support and help to the couple, must be regarded as delinquent.

Our investigations suggest that seminaries have made considerable improvements since the Blount and Boyle study (reported in *Pastoral Psychology*, December 1961), but that they still have a long way to go. Providing courses for wives, and/or counseling for couples in trouble, is just not enough.

Other advanced training programs for pastors, such as clinical pastoral education (CPE) and training in counseling, need also to be reexamined for their impact on clergy marriages. We have accumulated some evidence that these programs, good in themselves, can occasionally damage and even destroy marriages. The application of "systems theory" to marital interaction now makes it clear that when one partner in a marriage is involved in a program that produces significant personal growth and change, with the other partner uninvolved or excluded, alienation within the relationship is a frequent and sometimes fatal consequence.

III. Direct Services to Clergy Marriages

We have already referred to the need for these, but would like to spell it out in more detail.

What's Happening to Clergy Marriages?

(1) *Prevention and early detection of dysfunction.* We have made it very clear that most clergy marriages could be considerably improved and that marriage enrichment programs provide an excellent way of equipping couples to do this. We have seen that many of the denominations are beginning to offer such opportunities for enrichment.

However, we would urge that these programs be competent enough to be effective. The increasing popularity of marriage enrichment is spawning a number of inferior programs that, as some researchers are demonstrating, are ineffective. The Association of Couples for Marriage Enrichment (ACME) has kept a close watch on this field for several years, has established criteria for effective events, and has set standards for the selection, training, and certification of leader couples. (For a copy of the *Standards* document send a stamped address envelope to ACME, P.O. Box 10596, Winston-Salem, N.C. 27108.) It is simply irresponsible for a denomination to use leader couples who do not measure up to these standards, which are now being widely accepted.

There is still some hesitation among clergy couples to become involved in marriage enrichment. A great deal of encouragement can be given by subsidizing such participation. But the best way of all is for highly placed denominational leaders and their spouses to lead the way. A good example was set by Chief of Chaplains of the U.S. Air Force General Richard Carr; he and his wife took training as an ACME leader couple and led retreats for service personnel and their spouses.

(2) *Marriage counseling services.* The message should be strong and clear that, when a clergy couple find themselves in serious trouble, the denomination stands ready to offer counseling help; and that such help will protect the couple's privacy and, if necessary, include financial aid. Some of the denominations are already providing this kind of service. It will, however, not be fully effective until a climate is established in which the pastor concerned can ask for help as early as possible, in the confident assurance that no kind of judgment or censure will be involved.

Here again, professional competence needs to be maintained. Marriage and family counselors used by the denominations should be able to meet the standards for clinical membership of the American Association for Marriage and Family Therapy, whether or not they happen to have such membership.

(3) *Policies for clergy divorce.* The final breakdown of a clergy marriage is a tragedy for all concerned—the pastor, his wife, their children, the congregation, and the denomination. In the past such events were rare, but not for very healthy reasons. Everyone who has worked with couples in serious trouble, as we have for forty years, knows that a small percentage of all couples are so ill-suited to each other, or to the marriage relationship, that the

only sensible thing to do is to release them from their misery. To add judgment and rejection to their already heavy burden is a tragic denial of Christian compassion. Dr. James Doty, in a paper submitted to us by The United Methodist Church, quotes the experience of De Forest Wiksten, who as an area director dealt with thirty clergy marriages that ended in divorce. "I never saw one in which the pastor was irresponsible in approaching it. There was enormous pain, agony, and endless struggle to work through to a solution." One divorcing pastor was reported to us as having said, bitterly, "The Christian Church is the only army that shoots its wounded."

Most of the denominations are now busily framing policies for clergy divorce, and a good deal of material on this subject has come into our hands. We have not felt however that it belongs to this book. What we want to urge upon the churches is that there are plenty of clergy marriages that will be ripe for divorce in the coming years unless the kind of preventive services for which we are pleading are made available.

Again and again we have been asked for statistics about clergy divorces. Some of the denominations have made their own computations, and these can provide a rough indication of how the rates are increasing. However, we have heard some alarming figures quoted that cannot possibly be accurate, and we need to urge caution. To gain some perspective we personally consulted Dr. Paul Glick, Senior Demographer in the Population Division of the Bureau of Census in the federal government. He gave us all the figures he had. In 1960 the divorce rate for clergy was 0.2 percent. In 1970 it had doubled to 0.4 percent, but unfortunately in that year the figures for other religious workers were included with those for clergymen, confusing the issue. Further figures that can be relied upon will not be available until the 1980 census is completed.

IV. Clergy-Congregational Issues

We have already discussed a good many of the concerns in this area—congregational expectations, work schedules, salaries, housing and moving. We would add here only a brief discussion of two issues:

(1) *Contracts with congregations.* We have become increasingly convinced of the wisdom of a proposal made in our National Consultation on Clergy Marriage in 1977. The substance of it is that, before a pastor assumes charge of a congregation, he and his wife should sit down with representative church leaders and reach agreement about the many and various issues that need to be settled between them. Something like this is no doubt already done in many churches. But our proposal includes what appear to

be three new factors, all of which seem relevant and important. One is that the pastor's wife should share fully in the discussion, as a concerned party—although she may not personally be involved in the final contract. The second is that the discussion should be presided over by a skilled neutral negotiator, hired for the purpose if necessary. The third is that the contract should be renegotiated during each year of the pastorate and amended as necessary. An additional suggestion would be that a standard agenda might be prepared for negotiating these contracts.

We are convinced that there is considerable confusion about expectations and assumptions on the part of all the parties concerned—the pastor, his wife, their family, and the congregation—and that this causes an unnecessary degree of misunderstanding and even recrimination that might be greatly reduced by getting everything out into the open.

(2) *Pastoring clergy couples.* An issue that has frequently come to our attention is that clergy couples, in their relationship with their denominational colleagues and superiors, face the real or imagined risk of losing caste if they admit having marital difficulties. Again and again, we have found, they avoid making any open acknowledgment of their marital troubles until the conflicts are so far advanced that they may be beyond resolution. If some way could be found of providing regular contacts with a kind of *pastor pastorum*, someone who could be pledged to confidence and yet could guide them to an appropriate source of help, early detection of marital trouble could be greatly facilitated.

We are aware that denominational officials are ready to render this service. But their task is made difficult because in the hierarchy they hold the position of superiors. We are also aware that access to a designated conselor is sometimes made available. But again, unfortunately, going to a counselor is widely viewed as an action that carries with it a subtle stigma, because it suggests an admission of inadequacy and failure.

It may be that here the Protestant churches, in abandoning the confessional, have lost something that cannot be replaced in any other way. Yet it seems that someone like an *ombudsman*, but with rather different functions, could be appointed to keep in regular touch with all the clergy couples in a geographical area. He (or she) should be completely divested of all disciplinary and therapeutic functions and represent only a hearing ear and an understanding heart.

V. Varieties of Clergy Marriage

In this book we have been thinking mainly of the one-pastor-one-church ministry, which we believe represents the vast majority of clergy appointments. However, the functions of ministers are today widely diversified, and the implications for the clergy couple vary accordingly. Hunt has described a wide range of nonparish ministries: chaplains of many kinds; college campus teachers and administrators; seminary teachers; officials in denominational and ecumenical agencies; specialists in music, the arts, and communications; and others.

We would like to say a special word about *missionary* couples. When we worked for the World Council of Churches, we had many experiences on mission compounds where we were turned to by distracted couples who had found themselves in a desperate situation when they developed marital trouble. There was no one to confide in and nowhere to go for help. On one occasion we sat up nearly half the night and heard a tragic story. On another occasion we had to negotiate the sending home of a couple from a distant mission field; there was no other course possible in the circumstances.

For some years we served as consultants in family life to a center where missionaries were finally briefed before going abroad. We cannot speak too emphatically of the need, before any missionary couple go to the field, either for the first time or for a further term, to check out thoroughly the health of the marriage before they leave. We believe that nearly all missionaries would fully understand the importance of this and support the process even if they personally were not in need of it.

Finally, we would like to comment briefly on two quite new forms of clergy marriage that have made their appearance in recent years—the married clergywoman and her husband, and the two-clergy couple.

A woman minister, representing one of the denominations, took us to task because, in the questionnaire we sent out, no specific reference was made to women ministers. We are certainly not unaware of the increasing numbers of women who are now in the ministry. We welcome them, and we have ourselves for many years strongly supported their right to serve. However, they represent at present only a very small porportion of all ministers; and, what is decisive for us, we have been unable to find enough information about their married status, and the attitudes of their husbands, to present a clear or reliable picture. The only book we have found on the subject, that of the Proctors, is far too sensational to be a reliable guide. So we would offer the same plea as that which is printed on a folder issued by The Ministers' Life and Casualty Union: "This pamphlet is addressed to the problems of women married to male pastors. Not because female pastors do not exist. But because, as yet, there are far more ministers' wives than ministers' husbands. When the ratio changes, you can be sure Ministers' Life will study the new situation."

The other new form is what we call the two-clergy couple. An attempt has been made, as we indicated in the preface, to use the term "clergy couple" exclusively to describe this form of marriage. We consider this unwise, because it is only likely to lead to confusion.

An important consultation was held on October 30 to November 2, 1978, in Ohio, in which the concerns of two-clergy couples were thoroughly ventilated. The consultation was held under the auspices of the National Council of Churches (Professional Church Leadership), and a sophisticated report has been issued (von Lackum).

The report suggests that there may now be as many as six thousand two-clergy couples in all branches of Protestantism in the United States. True, this is only about 1 percent of all ordained clergy, but it would represent a higher percentage of all *married* clergy, since unmarried Catholic priests are included in the grand total. The evidence suggests, also, that the numbers are growing at a considerable rate. There are now seminaries where clergy couples in training make up nearly 50 percent of the entire student body.

The two-clergy couples are predominantly young, and they vary, individually and in their marital conditions, as widely as ministers generally vary. Their work patterns also vary widely. Following preparation for their lifework, some may be employed as co-pastors in the same church; some separately in different roles in the same church; some as pastors of different churches; some with one spouse serving as homemaker or in a secular occupation.

The Proctors in their book indicate that this new form of ministry can pose some knotty problems for the denominations, for the churches they serve and for the partners themselves. Yet ideally this could be for many couples a completely satisfying form of shared ministry, which sweeps away all the inequities and injustices of the past. It would truly represent the "companionship marriage" in action at the highest level of united service to others.

We were unable to include two-clergy couples in our investigation, for very much the same reasons as in the case of married clergywomen. The phenomenon is too new for reliable findings to be secured. But at least we would urge that its newness should not be a ground for prejudice or cynicism. To us, it seems to represent several important principles to which the churches have long needed to give more serious attention.

Summary

Here, briefly stated, is the substance of what we have tried to say in this book:

1. Clergy marriages today are breaking down in larger

numbers than ever before, and the rates are likely to increase.

2. A number of studies have shown that quite a large proportion of clergy couples are not satisfied with the conditions under which they have to live and work.

3. Examination of those conditions shows that some helpful changes could be made, both in the organization of the ministry and in the attitudes of both congregations and of clergy families to each other.

4. However, situational scene-shifting, though desirable, will not be enough. Our investigations suggest that the most serious difficulties in clergy marriages lie hidden within the interpersonal relationship of husband and wife.

5. These difficulties are substantially the same as those that couples generally are experiencing in our contemporary culture; but they are more serious for clergy couples because their expectations, and the expectations that congregations have for them, call for a higher standard than that of the secular society.

6. By good fortune, at this critical time new knowledge about intimate relationships and new resources for helping married couples to realize their expectations are becoming available.

7. It is therefore highly desirable that clergy couples, of all people, should welcome these new resources, use them in promoting their own relational growth, and then make them available to the couples in their congregations.

8. Denominational leaders and church officials need to understand the present crisis in clergy marriages, so that they can give enlightened support to the programs and policies that are called for at this time.

APPENDIX II

List of Sources

The following list is made up mainly of books and articles. However, a few unpublished dissertations and printed or mimeographed reports are also included.

These were the written resources we used in our preparation for writing our book. Most of the material we read in full, though sometimes only a chapter or section was relevant. In a few instances, we were unable to secure a copy of the item in time to use it, but, since we believe it represents relevant source material, we include it for the benefit of others who wish to explore the field.

We have listed all the materials together for easy identification by readers who wish to look up the sources of passages we have referred to or quoted.

Audet, Jean-Paul. *Structures of Christian Priesthood.* New York: The Macmillan Co., 1968.

Bader, Golda Elam, ed. *I Married a Minister.* Nashville: New York: Abingdon-Cokesbury Press, 1942.

Bailey, Robert and Mary Frances. *Coping with Stress in the Minister's Home.* Nashville: Broadman Press, 1979.

Bainton, Roland H. *Here I Stand: A Life of Martin Luther.* Nashville: New York: Abingdon-Cokesbury Press, 1950.

Bassett, William W., and Huizing, Peter J., eds. *Celibacy in the Church.* New York: The Seabury Press, 1972.

Beaven, A. W. *The Fine Art of Living Together.* New York: Harper & Brothers, 1927.

Blackwood, Andrew W. *Pastoral Work, A Source Book for Ministers.* Philadelphia: The Westminster Press, 1945.

Blackwood, Carolyn P. *The Pastor's Wife,* Philadelphia: The Westminster Press, 1951.

Blenkinsopp, Joseph. *Celibacy, Ministry, Church.* New York: Herder and Herder, 1968.

Blizzard, Samuel W. "The Minister's Dilemma." *The Christian Century,* April 25, 1956.

Blount, Louise Forman, and Boyle, John H. "The Theological Seminary and the Pastor's Wife." *Pastoral Psychology,* December 1961.

Bonnell, George C. "The Pastor's Wife: An Appeal to Fairness." *Pastoral Psychology*, December 1961.

Booth, Gotthard. *The Psychological Examination of Candidates for the Ministry*. Report on the Academy of Religion of Mental Health, New York City. n.d.

Bouma, Mary L. *Divorce in the Parsonage*. Bethany Fellowship Press, 6820 Auto Club Rd., Minneapolis, Mn. 55438, 1979.

Bowers, Margaretta K. *Conflicts of the Clergy: A Psychodynamic Study with Case Histories*. Nashville: Thomas Nelson, 1963.

Brett, Wesley E. "Marriage, Divorce and Remarriage in the Writings of Martin Luther." Dissertation, Wake Forest University, 1977.

Bridges, Charles. *The Christian Ministry: With an Enquiry Into the Causes of Its Inefficiency*. New York: R. Carter & Brothers, 1868 (originally 1829).

Brown, Jerry. "Pastoral Care—Of, by, and for the Minister's Family." *The Quarterly Review of Southern Baptist Progress*, Oct., Nov., Dec., 1977.

Child, Frank S. *The Colonial Parson of New England*. Detroit: Gale Research Co., 1974 (originally 1896).

Christmas, Frederick E. *The Parson in English Literature*. London: Hodder & Stoughton, 1950.

Clinebell, Charlotte Holt. *Meet Me in the Middle: On Becoming Human Together*. New York: Harper & Row, 1973.

Clinebell, Charlotte H. and Howard J. *The Intimate Marriage*. New York: Harper & Row, 1970.

Clinebell, Howard J. "Interview on the Minister's Family." *The Christian Ministry*, July 1971.

Croskery, Beverly. "The Wife's View of Parish Life." *The Christian Ministry*, January 1977.

Davies, Horton. *A Mirror of the Ministry in Modern Novels*. London: Oxford University Press, 1959.

Deen, Edith. *Family Living in the Bible*. New York: Harper & Row, 1963.

Denton, Wallace. "New Look at a Familiar Face." *Pastoral Psychology*, December 1961.

———. "Role Attitudes of the Minister's Wife." *Pastoral Psychology*, December 1961.

———. *The Role of the Minister's Wife*. Philadephia: The Westminster Press, 1962.

———. *The Minister's Wife as a Counselor*. Philadelphia: The Westminster Press, 1966.

Dittes, James E. *Minister on the Spot*. Philadelphia: Pilgrim Press, 1970.

Dodds, Elizabeth D. "The Minister's Homemaker." *Pastoral Psychology*, September 1960.

Doty, James. *Working with Clergy Families in Trouble*. Report presented at Methodist Council of Bishops Seminar Meeting, Oklahoma City, March 27-31, 1978.

Douglas, William. "Ministers' Wives: A Tentative Typology." *Pastoral Psychology*, December 1961.

———. "Minister and Wife: Growth in Relationship."*Pastoral Psychology*, December 1961.

———. *Ministers' Wives*. New York: Harper & Row, 1965.

Dykes, James Oswald. *The Christian Minister and His Duties*. Edinburgh: T. & T. Clark, 1908.

Eliot, George. *Scenes of Clerical Life*. Edited by David Lodges. Baltimore: Penguin Books, 1973 (originally 1858).

Fairchild, Roy Warren, and Wynn, J. C. *Families in the Church: A Protestant Survey*. New York: Association Press, 1961.

Fisher, Welthy H. *Handbook for Ministers' Wives*. New York: Woman's Press, 1950.

Fosdick, Harry Emerson. *The Living of These Days: An Autobiography*. New York: Harper & Brothers, 1956.

Frein, George H., ed. *Celibacy: The Necessary Option*. New York: Herder and Herder, 1968.

Galbraith, Lois Hall. "The Established Clergy as Depicted in English Prose Fiction in 1740—1800." Dissertation, University of Pennsylvania, 1950 (privately printed).

Goldsmith, Oliver. *The Vicar of Wakefield*. New York: Modern Library, 1955 (originally 1780).

Gordon, Huntly. *The Minister's Wife*. Boston: Routledge & Kegan Paul, 1978.

Graybeal, David M. *The Christian Family and Its Money*. Pamphlet, Drew University, Madison, N.J., n.d. (privately printed).

Harmon, Nolan B. *Ministerial Ethics and Etiquette*. Nashville: Cokesbury Press, 1928.

Hart, A. Tindal. *The Country Priest in English History*. London: Phoenix House, 1959.

Hayes, Kenneth E. *The Critical Needs of Pastors*. Report of the Research Services Department, Sunday School Board, Southern Baptist Convention, Nashville, Tenn., June 1976.

———. *Pastors' Wives Survey*. Report of the Research Services Department, Sunday School Board, Southern Baptist Convention, Nashville, Tenn., July 1976.

Hewitt, Arthur Wentworth. *The Shepherdess*. New York: Willett, Clark & Co., 1943.

Hiltner, Seward. "Divorced Ministers." *Pastoral Psychology*. December 1961.

Hobkirk, Marietta B. "Some Reflections on Bringing Up the Minister's Family." *Pastoral Psychology*, December 1961.

Hollis, Harry N., Jr., ed., with Vera and David Mace and Sarah Frances Anders. *Christian Freedom for Women: And Other Human Beings*. Nashville: Broadman Press, 1975.

Houts, Donald C. "Pastoral Care for Pastors: Toward a Church Strategy." *Pastoral Psychology,* Spring 1977.

Howell, John C. *Equality and Submission in Marriage.* Nashville: Broadman Press, 1979.

Hulme, William E. "The Seminary Student and His Family Life." *Pastoral Psychology,* Sepember 1960.

Hunt, Richard A. *Ministry and Marriage.* Ministry Studies Board, P.O. Box 8265, Dallas, Tex., 1976.

———. *Clergy Families Under Stress.* Report presented at the Seminar on Clergy Marriage and Divorce, Council of Bishops, The United Methodist Church, Oklahoma City Meeting, March 28, 1978.

Jarvis, Kathleen. *The Impressions of a Parson's Wife.* London: A. R. Mowbray & Co. Ltd., 1951.

Johnson, Anna F. *The Making of a Minister's Wife.* New York: Appleton-Century-Crofts, 1939.

Kaiser, Beverly. "The Role of the Minister's Wife in the Local Church." Dissertation, School of Education, Boston University, 1958.

Knox-Little, W. J. *Holy Matrimony.* London: Longman, Green, Ltd., 1900.

Koehler, John G. "The Minister as a Family Man." *Pastoral Psychology,* September 1960.

Küng, Hans. *Why Priests?* Garden City, N. Y.: Doubleday & Co., 1972.

Lamont, Thomas W. *My Boyhood in a Parsonage.* New York: Harper & Brothers, 1946.

Lavender, Lucille. *They Cry, Too! What You Always Wanted to Know About Your Minister But Didn't Know Whom to Ask.* New York: Hawthorn Books, 1976.

Lea, Henry C. *History of Sacerdotal Celibacy in the Christian Church.* London: Watts and Co., 1932.

McDaniel, Douglass Scarborough. *The Pastor's Helpmate.* Nashville: Broadman Press, 1942.

McGinnis, Thomas C. "Clergymen in Conflict." *Pastoral Psychology,* October 1969.

Mace, David and Vera. *We Can Have Better Marriages If We Really Want Them.* Nashville: Abingdon, 1974.

———. *Marriage Enrichment in the Church.* Nashville: Broadman Press, 1976.

———. *How to Have a Happy Marriage.* Nashville: Abingdon, 1977.

Mattis, Mary. *Pastors' Wives Study.* Report of Research Division of the Support Agency, United Presbyterian Church, New York, 1977.

Menges, Robert J., and Dittes, J. E. *Psychological Studies of Clergymen.* Nashville: Thomas Nelson, 1965.

Middleton, Robert J. "A Way of Family Living." *The Christian Ministry*, July 1971.

Miller, Althea S. *Under the Parsonage Roof*. Chicago: Moody Press, 1969.

Morentz, Paul E. "The Image of the Seminary Wife." *Pastoral Psychology*, December 1961.

Nelson, Martha. *This Call We Share*. Nashville: Broadman Press, 1977.

Nelson, Wesley W. *Crying for My Mother: The Intimate Life of a Clergyman*. Chicago: Covenant Press, 1975.

Niebuhr, H. Richard, and Williams, Daniel D., eds. *The Ministry in Historical Perspectives*. New York: Harper & Brothers, 1956.

Nordland, Frances. *The Unprivate Life of a Pastor's Wife*. Chicago: Moody Press, 1972.

Nyberg, Kathleen Neill. *The Care and Feeding of Ministers*. Nashville: Abingdon, 1961.

Oates, Wayne. *The Minister's Own Mental Health*. New York: Channel Press, 1955.

O'Brien, John A., ed. *Why Priests Leave: The Intimate Stories of 12 Who Did*. New York: Hawthorn Books, 1969.

Oden, Marilyn Brown. *The Minister's Wife: Person or Position?* Nashville: Abingdon, 1966.

————. "Updating the Minister's Wife." *The Christian Ministry*, January 1977.

O'Neill, David P. *Priestly Celibacy and Maturity*. New York: Sheed and Ward, 1965.

Otto, Herbert A., ed. *Marriage and Family Enrichment: New Perspectives and Programs*. Nashville: Abingdon, 1976.

Padwick, Constance E. *Temple Gairdner of Cairo*. New York: The Macmillan Co., 1929.

Palmer, Albert W. *The Minister's Job*. Chicago: Willett, Clark & Co., 1937.

Parker, T.H.L. *Portrait of Calvin*. London: SCM Press, 1954.

Parrott, Lora Lee. *How to Be a Preacher's Wife and Like It*. Grand Rapids: Zondervan Publishing House, 1956.

Pentecost, Dorothy. *The Pastor's Wife and the Church*. Chicago: Moody Press, 1964.

Prasse, Barbara. "The Changing Role of the Minister's Wife." *The Christian Ministry*, July 1971.

Presnell, William B. "Clergy Marriage and Its Significance for Ministry." Dissertation, Drew University, 1976.

————. "The Minister's Own Marriage." *Pastoral Psychology*, Summer 1977.

Proctor, Priscilla and William. *Women in the Pulpit: Is God an Equal Opportunity Employer?* Garden City, N. Y.: Doubleday & Co., 1976.

Purkiser, W.T., *The New Testament Image of the Ministry*. Kansas City: Beacon Hill Press, 1969.

Ragsdale, Ray W. *The Mid-Life Crises of a Minister.* Waco, Tex: Word Books, 1978.

Rankin, Robert Parks. "The Ministerial Calling and the Minister's Wife." *Pastoral Psychology*, September 1960.

Rediger, G. Lloyd. "Mirages in the Pastor's Marriage." *The Christian Ministry*, July 1971.

Roberts, Evelyn. *His Darling Wife, Evelyn: The Autobiography of Mrs. Oral Roberts.* New York: Damascus House, 1976.

Scanzoni, John. "Role Incompatibility in Clergy Marriages." Dissertation, University of Oregon, 1964.

————. "Resolution of Occupational-Conjugal Role Conflict in Clergy Marriages." *Journal of Marriage and the Family*, August 1965.

Schillebeeckx, Edward. *Clerical Celibacy Under Fire: A Critical Appraisal.* New York: Sheed and Ward, 1968.

Schroer, Ann and Hale. "Strengths and Strains of a Parsonage Marriage." *The Christian Ministry*, July 1971.

Smith, Thomas R. "The Pastor-Husband and Wife." Dissertation, Florida State University, 1976.

Spence, Hartzell. *One Foot in Heaven.* New York: McGraw-Hill Book Co., 1940.

Stark, Phyllis. *I Chose a Parson.* London: Oxford University Press, 1956.

Stewart, Charles William. *Person and Profession: Career Development in the Ministry.* Nashville: Abingdon, 1974.

Stylites, Simeon. "A New Look in Preachers' Wives." *The Christian Century*, December 21, 1955.

Tavard, George H. *Woman in Christian Tradition.* Notre Dame, Ind: University of Notre Dame Press, 1973.

Taylor, Alice. *How to Be a Minister's Wife and Love it.* Grand Rapids: Zondervan Publishing House, 1968.

Taylor, Mary G. "Two-Person Career or Two-Career Marriage?" *The Christian Ministry*, January 1977.

Tracy, Wesley D. "Wasted Wives." *The Preachers' Magazine*, February 1963.

Trollope, Anthony. *Barchester Towers.* New York: Harcourt Brace Jovanovich, 1962 (originally 1857).

Troutner, Ernest John. "Optimal Factors in Marital Decision—Making with 140 Methodists Ministers and Their Wives." Dissertation, School of Theology, Boston University, 1961.

Truman, Ruth. *Underground Manual for Ministers' Wives.* Nashville: Abingdon, 1974.

van Arnold, William. "Husband-Wife Interaction of Selected Theological Students." Dissertation, Southern Baptist Theological Seminary, Louisville, Ky., 1970.

von Lackum, John P., III, and Nancy Jo Kemper. *A Report on Clergy Couples Consultation* (dealing with two-clergy cou-

60722

ples only). Professional Church Leadership, National Council of Churches, New York, March 15, 1979.

Walker, D. D. *The Human Problems of the Minister.* New York: Harper & Brothers, 1960.

Watt, Margaret. *The History of the Parson's Wife.* London: Faber & Faber, 1943.

Wynn, John Charles. *Pastoral Ministry to Families.* Philadelphia: The Westminster Press 1957.

———. "Consider the Children." *Pastoral Psychology,* September 1960.

———. "Pastors Have Family Problems Too." *Pastoral Psychology,* September 1960.

Yearbook of American and Canadian Churches. Pamphlet, National Council of Churches of Christ in the U.S.A., New York, 1979.